How to Deal With Everything

A Guide to a Stress-Free and Happy Life

To Anna,

Thank you for creating an environment that I look forward to each day and for the invaluable example you set. Your leadership is a breath of fresh air, bringing clarity and purpose to our work.
This book is but a small token of my gratitude for all you do.

Silviu Pristavu

Copyright © 2024 Silviu Pristavu
For reproduction, distribution and translation, please write us at silviu@arenes.pro

All rights reserved

ISBN: 979-8-3377-2028-9

Contents

Preface	1
1: Why we're doing what we're doing	5
2: Attitude	23
3: The Mirror Effect	34
4: Love	43
5: Forgiveness	51
6: The Golden Rule	57
7: Tools to Use When Dealing with Everything	69
- Affirmations	69
- Education	79
- Exercise	83
- Gratitude	85
- Ho'oponopono	93
- Mindfulness	96
- Incorporating these tools into your daily life	100
Afterword	106
Acknowledgements	108
References	109

Preface

Do you want to be happy? Of course you do. Who doesn't? But what exactly is happiness? Take a look at kids. Do they seem happy? Do they act happy? Absolutely. Why? Because they live entirely in the moment. They're fully present in whatever they're doing, with days filled with pure, unfiltered joy. They embrace each moment without distraction, diving into one game without worrying about the next. We've all wished, at least once, to go back to that carefree, stress-free time of childhood. Wouldn't that be something? If you've ever longed to recapture that childlike sense of wonder, living fully in the present, while still handling adult responsibilities, then this book might just be the guide you've been looking for.

For years, I've worked as a delivery driver for various online retailers. In many cases, I'm the only human interaction that customers have during their entire buying experience. I take real pride in this role, ensuring every delivery comes with a smile. While my paycheck doesn't reflect that of a CEO, I approach my job with the same level of commitment and enthusiasm, treating each customer with genuine appreciation. This attitude not only makes people feel valued but has also earned me a few nicknames like "Mr. Happy," "Happy Face," or "Mr. Smiley."

Whether it's early in the morning or late in the evening, whether I'm loading and unloading at the depot or out on the road, I always greet people with a smile. And whenever someone asks, "How're you doing?" my answer is always the same – "I'm living the dream!"

At first, I'm sure many thought I was being sarcastic, forgot my meds, or maybe took them all at once. I didn't just assume this from their puzzled expressions. A colleague once told me, "I think you're full of s**t; nobody can be this happy all the time." More often, I'd get asked, "What do you take with your coffee?" But over time, as people saw me consistently upbeat day after day, they have realized that this is who I am at my core. And, to my delight, they've come to enjoy seeing me around.

I remember when I started my latest route; there was a customer who greeted me with a sour, grumpy face the first time I knocked on their door. They opened it with a sharp "What?" that sent shivers down my spine. Despite their demeanor, I handed over the parcel with a smile and said, "Have a wonderful day!" – only to have the door slammed in my face.

Weeks went by, and I kept returning, not by choice but because they kept ordering online. With every visit, I continued to smile and wish them a wonderful day. Slowly but surely, their attitude began to change. One day, when they heard my signature knock, they opened the door with a smile that melted my heart and brought tears of joy to my soul.

That moment wasn't just the highlight of my day; it was a powerful reminder that people can change when met with kindness, love, and a smile. Today, their happiness fuels mine and motivates me to keep going. People are influenced by kindness just as much as they are by negativity. Whether you take out your frustrations on others or show them your positive, happy side, your actions affect their mood, and ultimately, those actions come back to you. This alone should be enough reason for those of us who still have hope for a better world not to give up.

I want to help make this world a better place for us and future generations, a place where people live and work in harmony, love each other regardless of origin or skin color, and accept one another with all our unique quirks. A borderless world where we share this brief moment in the life of the universe equally, without wasting it on conflicts over things that neither last nor matter in the grand scheme.

This is my mission. I know that change doesn't happen forcefully or overnight, and I respect every individual's free will and their own version of happiness. For those who haven't yet found their balance, I want to share my life experiences and happiness through the words in this book.

My hope is that they will inspire you to follow your bliss and find the frequency that resonates most deeply with your being.

1: Why We're Doing What We're Doing

The environment shapes people's actions and behaviors. It is the invisible hand that guides us.
—James Clear[1]

From the moment we are born, our minds begin absorbing information like parched land soaking up the first drops of rain after a long drought. Everything around us – sounds, colors, smells, tastes, and sensations – is stored in the most powerful hard drive known to humanity: our brains. This raw data is then processed by our minds, transforming into small programs we call beliefs: grass is green unless it's dry, fruits are sweet unless they're unripe, ice is cold, and animals have distinctive smells.

As our minds evolve, we learn the language, habits, and peculiarities of the people in the community where we grow. In this process, our minds adopt these languages, habits, and peculiarities as a way to blend in and be accepted. When a "free spirit" attempts to break away from these communal norms, they're often "corrected" by others with the wisdom of experience – "That's not how we do things around here. This is how it's done!" If you have children, you probably find yourself trying to teach them to do things "the right way," don't you?

Every community, whether it's a family, religious group, neighborhood, or nation, has created and "perfected" over time what they consider to be "the best way to live." They are rarely shy about sharing these views with a "newcomer." This young mind, knowing nothing beyond its own experiences, often adopts this information to the point of developing what we might call "blind beliefs."

There is an urban legend, its earliest mention being in Gary Hamel and C.K. Prahalad book Competing for the Future[2], where, in a hypothetical experiment, a researcher places four monkeys in a cage. Inside the cage, a bunch of bananas hangs from a string, with a set of stairs leading up to it. Before long, one monkey goes to the stairs and starts climbing toward the bananas. The moment it touches the bananas, the researcher sprays all the monkeys with ice-cold water.

After a while, another monkey tries to climb the stairs, and again, all the monkeys are doused with ice-cold water. When a third monkey makes an attempt, as soon as its foot touches the stairs, the others, fearing another cold shower, physically prevent it from climbing.

At this point, the researcher removes the cold water from the experiment and replaces one of the original monkeys with a new one. The newcomer, seeing the bananas, starts to climb the stairs, but to its surprise and horror, the other three monkeys attack it. After a few more attempts, the new monkey learns that climbing the stairs will result in an assault, though it doesn't understand why.

The researcher then replaces another of the original four monkeys with a new one. Predictably, the newcomer tries to climb the stairs and is attacked. The previous newcomer, now fully integrated into the group, joins in the punishment with enthusiasm. This process continues until all the original monkeys have been replaced.

At this stage, none of the monkeys remaining in the cage have ever been sprayed with cold water, yet they continue to prevent any monkey from climbing the stairs. Why? Because as far as they know, that's just the way it's always been done.

People often behave in the same way. How many times have you heard the phrase, "It's always been done this way. Don't mess with what works"? Instead of challenging these assumptions, many of us, like the monkeys, simply continue to reproduce what has been done before. It's the path of least resistance.

We inherit beliefs from our communities – beliefs that even they may not fully understand. Yet, because these beliefs were passed down in a certain way, they go unchallenged.

The point I want to make is that we are products of our environments to a certain extent. The language we speak, the culture we embrace, the religion we follow, and the food we eat – these are not our choices; we've been "educated" into them, and they become part of who we are. And that's fine until we look at the world and see nations at war for generations, where the people fighting no longer remember why they hate each other, but they continue to do so, blindly, for their country.

According to Maslow's hierarchy of needs[3], our actions are driven by the level we find ourselves at during different stages in life. At the base level, our motivations are physiological, rooted in survival: food, water, shelter, health, warmth, and rest. Once these needs are met, our motivation shifts to safety. There's comfort in feeling safe and secure, whether it's the locks on our doors, a secure job, or living in a peaceful country. This security allows us to move to the next level – belonging. Here, being loved becomes our primary motivator. We seek social connections, crave interaction, and need friendship, family, intimacy, and love.

Once we feel a sense of belonging, our needs evolve to the esteem level. At this stage, we strive for recognition, status, and respect, whether it's respect from others or self-respect. These are the forces driving us forward. Finally, once all these needs are satisfied, we reach the

[margin note: Being understood? Which is that?]

==level of self-actualization== – the pursuit of our full potential. At this stage, we aim to become the best we can possibly be.

As you read through these stages, you might be trying to identify the level you're at in your life right now. But here's what I think – This isn't just the level you're at in life; it's the level your mind is at. We are not our minds. We are the consciousness, the beings who live within bodies enriched by minds that we educate and elevate as we navigate life. No matter which level your mind is at, YOU can consciously choose your motivations. You can be a CEO at the self-actualization level and still act on base impulses in certain situations. Or you could be homeless yet spend your days reading in libraries, nourishing your mind. While our environments shape our minds and raise us through the different levels, ==it's the conscious choices we make that distinguish between our habitual minds and our true selves.==

In our daily routines, many actions are done automatically. We often find ourselves moving through the day unconsciously, only to realize hours later that we can't remember where the time has gone. Days blur into weeks, months, and years. We come to realize that our comfort zones, while cozy, keep us stuck in a stagnant stage. Some people, when they eventually recognize that their lives have been nothing more than a series of instinctual decisions, take action to change. But the majority, even when they become aware, fear breaking the cycle. No matter how mundane their life may be, it's familiar; it's something they know and can predict.

I love the way Don Miguel Ruiz puts it in his book The Four Agreements:

> *Suffering makes you feel safe because you know it so well, but there's really no reason to suffer. The only reason you suffer is because you choose to suffer. If you look at your life you'll find many excuses to suffer, but a good reason to suffer you will not find. The same is true for happiness. The only reason you're happy is because you choose to be happy. Happiness is a choice and so is suffering.*[4]

So, people only change when their environment forces them to, when they are pushed to either move up or regress, depending on their courage to break through the fear barrier that holds them back.

One perspective is that we are products of our environments and that whatever happens around us determines who we are and what we become. My opinion is that we are, indeed, but only to the extent that we allow it. We become products of our environments when our minds are so desperate to fit in that they conform to that environment's norms and expectations. We are products of our environments as long as our habitual minds control every aspect of our lives. Our minds absorb information from the environments and simply replicate it. It classifies what it learns as good or bad, safe or unsafe, using that information to predict outcomes. What it doesn't know, it controls with fear – the mind's refusal to navigate uncharted waters and situations where it cannot predict the outcome. If left in charge, our minds would forbid us from trying anything new, keeping us confined to the bubble of knowledge it has gathered.

Every decision we make in spite of our fears pushes us out of the comfort zones of our minds. Every choice that diverges from our habitual lives makes us a product of our decisions, not our environments. We are what we decide to be. Yes, our minds may resist at first, screaming and flooding our bodies with fear, shame, and guilt for not following the path "we're supposed to walk."

How many times have you held back on your desires because you feared your parents wouldn't approve, society would frown upon your actions, or your friends would judge you? Every time you did so, you reverted to being a product of that environment, driven by the fear of judgment, exclusion, and becoming an outcast. This fear is the mind's response to its limited information. But when we break through the mind's limitations and step into new realms of knowledge, the mind has no choice but to adapt, absorbing the new information into its library and incorporating it into its programming. It is Your decision, Your will to step out of your mind's comfort zone; that is what makes you unique.

You have absolute power over your mind and, through that, over your entire life. You can train and retrain your mind to be and act as you wish. You can choose to let your mind control your daily routine, habits, reactions, and decisions, allowing it to make you feel miserable. Or you can step into a new field, one that you choose, where you feel free and happy. When the mind is in control, it's not about what you **want** to do or say, but it's what you feel you **have** to do because the environment dictates it. You have to go to work, even if you hate it. You have to pretend to be someone you're not to fit into a particular group, even though you know that's not who you are. The fear of not belonging, of not being loved and appreciated, makes your mind force you into actions that don't align with your true self.

But here's what you're missing – if you allow yourself to be YOU, not only will you feel better about yourself and experience genuine happiness, but you'll also start attracting people who appreciate you for who you really are; the joyful, unique, and quirky being you truly are, rather than who you pretend to be. This way, you get to be loved, accepted, and appreciated for your true self. You don't have to pretend to be someone else to fit in. You can be who you are and fit where it feels right.

Seven years ago, whilst under employment, I got promoted to operations manager and I was really excited about it. One of the things that got me there was my willingness to defeat limitations and break down barriers. Another thing, and probably the most important one, was my attitude. I was always glowing and happy, and instead of wishing people a good day, I was wishing them a wonderful day. A few months later, a new general manager took charge of the service station, and shortly after he was installed, he took me to the side and explained to me that I was now in a managerial position and I had to tone down my excitement to show seriosity because if I'm going to keep going like that, people will treat me like a joke. "Oh, and about that 'Have a wonderful day' – don't use it that often. After a while it becomes boring and meaningless," he said to me.

I have to say that was the biggest blow I've received. The idea of holding on to my will to manifest myself freely made me miserable. I was no longer laughing in his presence; I barely joked around at work and when I did so, it made me feel guilty. From here onward, a downward spiral started rolling. My excitement and my genuinely expressed happiness had helped me climb through three positions within a year, but within another year, little by little, I grew to hate my job and hate waking up for work. I was no longer excited to do stuff, but "I had to" because it paid the bills. I wasn't suitable for a similar position in other companies because I didn't have enough experience due to my fast promotions. All my job applications were ignored or rejected, and the downward spiral kept rolling until one day I felt so exhausted that I requested a couple of days off to relax and detach.

For the first day, I sat on the couch watching numbing TV shows that were taking my mind away from work. Late in the evening, the out-of-hours team called me, probably because they had some issue that needed to be sorted by a manager and for whatever reason they called me on my day off. When I heard that phone ring and saw the number that was calling me, my body became sick instantly. I felt a pit in my stomach and a huge urge to vomit. Tears started rolling down my face in disgust and frustration. I felt like smashing that phone into a million pieces to make it stop.

My wife came to check up on me and I explained what I was going through, so she suggested I quit the job, but my mind kept bringing up those damned bills and all the reasons I shouldn't do this because I worked so hard to get so far and I could miss out on the opportunity of being promoted again. But the pain was too big; it was hurting too much, so in the end I decided to quit the job. All of my second day off I planned on how I would tell my boss that

I was leaving. On Friday, as I walked into the office, I asked my manager to see me in the meeting room, and once there I told him "I quit." The look on his face was one of confusion. He didn't see this coming and didn't know how to react.

I stayed there for six more weeks, but I allowed myself to be me again. The relaxation and joy that filled me during those weeks made me want to stay because it felt so good to be me again, though I knew it wouldn't be like that if I decided to stay. It would go back to what it was before my breakdown, so sadly that had to be the end of that chapter.

The moral of this story is that I became a product of that environment, controlled by it and by the one who I thought would help, as he promised, to get me promoted and climb up the career ladder. I don't know what other people would have done in my situation, but what I do know is that I decided to stop being chained to some promises, and stop being a gear in someone else's plans. I decided to free myself from pain and be myself once again – the joyful man who wishes everyone a wonderful day!

During high school, I tried to fit in with the cool kids. One of the things that, in my mind, made them cool and rebellious was the fact that they were smoking, and that was one thing I could do as well so I could relate and connect with them. I still remember the disgust I felt when

I inhaled the cigarette smoke for the first time; it even made me so dizzy that I lost my balance. That didn't stop me. My motivation to fit in was stronger than that and I thought, *If they can, I can*. It soon turned into a habit, and by the time I went to University, I was smoking up to forty cigarettes a day. As money management wasn't my strong suit at that time, I found myself one day having to choose between smoking another day or eating another week. So then and there I decided that I would stop smoking for good, and I did. I haven't had a cigarette since I made that decision.

As you can see, in both situations I had reached a very low point where I was forced to make a decision that would take me out of misery or help me survive with dignity. The stories you hear "from rags to riches" and "from homeless to millionaire" are all true because when we reach rock-bottom, the lowest point in our lives, something within us awakes – something that is beyond our minds comes into play. You see, when we allow our minds to control every aspect of our lives, we, as conscious beings, forget that we have the ability to choose. We become products of habits and of the environment, and we allow ourselves to float aimlessly to the point that we begin to believe that everything happens to us, and that we have no control.

"This is who I am," "This always happens to me," and "There is nothing I can do" are just a few of the things people say when they feel that they no longer have control over their lives. So it's no wonder that when these people hear me say, "You have control over every aspect of your life and your environment; you can decide what happens next and you can control your future," they start laughing out loud. Their mind does not have the ability to "see" what it didn't learn. Their mind's information is limited to their life experience. So when that mind controls all aspects of someone's life, it is only logical that they wouldn't be able to comprehend what I mean. That so-called victimhood mentality controls their lives and leaves them powerless in front of decision-making. And for as long as it is bearable, no matter how bad and frustrating it can be, and as long as it is predictable for their mind, those people will keep on living like that, unless they reach a critical point in their lives when they are forced to make a life-changing decision, or if they pick up a book like this and choose to take control of their life.

The comfort zones of our minds are our very own prisons. Everything that happens within these walls feels comfortable. Every time we step out of it, whether it's for an exam, an interview, a first date, jumping from a plane, and so on, our minds trigger the emergency lockdown protocol by spiking our thoughts with all the worst scenarios and our bodies with fear chemicals. Our minds need to protect themselves and the only thing that is keeping them alive – because if the body dies, the mind ceases to exist. So it's only natural for them to keep us from going out of our comfort zones. This is all good until it isn't. The mind doesn't feel the pain; it only triggers it. Our bodies are the things feeling pain, sickness, and frustrations, and that's why there's always this conflict between what should be done and what our minds dictate.

It is so much easier to choose the known path, and in all fairness, it's not much of a choice. It's the programming of our minds that can show us the end result, the "guarantee" of a set destination. The conditioning of our minds – that cozy blanket of our comfort zones – ensures that for as long as we are in a "good" position, we don't have to change things, hence the expression, "If it's not broken it doesn't need fixing." The only problem is that "good" is relative according to each individual's experience, and our minds would rather hold on to that good rather than let it go for a promise of "greater." Though we feel that we can do more, be more, and have more, our minds will always argue that we may lose what we have in order to stop us from reaching out of our comfort zones. Though what the mind doesn't know is that ==in order to have the better, we have to let go of the good.==

Understanding that we are not our minds is the first step in taking control of our lives. **We've been gifted with a mind, not enslaved with one.** Once this box is ticked, we can confidently say, "I am the master of my life. I am the master of my mind. I have control over my actions and control over my reactions. I am the one true captain of my life and I assume full responsibility for what happens around me."

If you find it hard to say these words because your mind's arguments point to a chaotic world where we have no control over what happens in our lives, I challenge you to do the following exercise – before going to sleep tonight, take a pen and paper and think of the worst way your following day can go. Write it down and go to sleep. The following day, in the evening, go through the list and see how many of those bad things have happened. Now take a new piece of paper and think of the best way your next day can go, and write them down. In the evening of the next day, come back to that piece of paper and tick all the things that happened. I get the feeling you already know deep within you that a huge chunk of the things you'll write down will become your reality, and you do know deep inside that you do have control over your life and over your environment. But if you don't, just take on the exercise and then come back to this book.

~

Now that you understand You are the master of your life, there is only one more obstacle between what you want and what you'll get, and that is your mind. You see, the mind is but a software that runs little programs in the background, which we call habits. In order to get the mind on your side, all you have to do is reprogram that software one habit at a time. Start with the little things, like the way you start your day, and change the order of the things you do. So, if the first thing you do when the alarm goes off is head to the bathroom and brush your teeth, try to mix it up a bit. Instead, before getting out of bed, think of five things that you are grateful for, then when you go to the bathroom, mix the order of the things you're doing. Do the same with getting dressed. If you usually put your left sock on first, start with the right one, or with any other garments you're putting on, try and change the order you put them on them. Or how you have your breakfast, or what you're having, or the things you do on the way to work, or the journey, and so on.

The most important thing that happens when you take control of the little things is that you become conscious of the things you're doing. You're no longer a tool of your mind's habits – you are now in charge of the things you're doing. Being conscious of your actions is the most important part of the process, and if you consistently try doing things differently every day, you train your mind that You are now in charge, you break the patterns, and you help your mind ease off. Then when you feel ready, you can start taking charge of a bigger habit and decide to put a stop to it. In 2020, I decided to stop eating meat for two months, and it was only because I could not see myself sitting down for a meal and not having a piece of meat on my plate. I was addicted to meat, so I challenged myself to tackle one of my biggest habits, since smoking was no longer in the picture, thinking that if I can do this I can do anything. I ended up not eating meat for two years.

On the other hand, you can start a brand new habit that will improve your life. There was a time when I wasn't good at managing my finances, so I was struggling a lot to make ends meet. And I read in a book, *The Richest Man in Babylon*,[5] that saving ten percent of your income is one very important step in taking control and increasing your wealth. So, I decided that for every amount that goes into my account, ten percent will be moved into savings. Yes, I was struggling, but because I made up my mind that I would save this money, I started looking into other ways to cut costs to make ends meet, and at the same time my savings were increasing, and slowly but surely, my control over my finances started shaping in my favor.

We can take control of our lives by taking control of our habits. Decide what you want or who you want to be, and as you go through your daily activity, observe your habits. Take them one by one and put them through the filter of your end goal – "Does this define the person I am at the end of my journey?" "Is this something the future me would do when I have reached the end goal?" Think of yourself as the person who has already achieved that goal.

Which of those habits would you still do in this position? James Clear, the author of *Atomic Habits*,[1] recently launched an app called *Atoms – from Atomic Habits*. It's free to download on your phone from Google Play if you're using Android, or the App Store if using iOS, and it will help you set and implement new goals in your daily routine. This way you'll be able to take control of the little things that control your life and, in the end, you'll be able to say that you're no longer a product of your environment but a product of your own choices, that you are your own creation.

2: Attitude

If with a pure mind a person speaks or acts, happiness follows him like his never-departing shadow.

—Buddha[6]

Your attitude sets the tone for the day. It may be impacted by the little things that happen while you're still in the process of awakening, but ultimately you have a choice to let life follow its course or take matters into your own hands and swerve it to serve your purpose. Life has this ability to spiral things. Whether it starts with a stubbed toe followed by a pigeon dropping on your brand new coat and ending in the loss of a job or a car accident, or it starts with a thought of deep gratitude that leads to free coffee, a promotion, and other amazing things. Either way, it's the magnetic ability of our minds that dictates which course the spiraling takes. ==What we focus on the most becomes our realities, so by deliberately choosing our thoughts, we choose our realities.== *Reframing a bad situation?*

We can either be products of our environments or products of our choices. By not making a deliberate choice, our minds observe the world around us – what we see, hear, smell, taste, and feel – and they create thoughts of their own. Those thoughts, in return, will bring about more of the same environment to be observed, and that's how the spiraling goes. If we are surrounded by sick people, our minds observe sick people, think about sick people, and bring about sickness in our lives. If we are surrounded by misery, our minds observe misery, think about misery, and bring about misery in our lives. If we are surrounded by wealthy people, our minds observe wealth, think about wealth, and bring about wealth in our lives. By choosing the kind of thoughts that dominate our conscious thinking, we choose the trajectory of our day-to-day lives. If we are surrounded by sick people and choose to be grateful for our health in those moments and look for ways we can help the sick people, we direct our focus toward health, which brings about health in our lives. If we are surrounded by misery, we can choose to be grateful for the little we have, dream of living a better life, and in this way we bring about more opportunities to choose a better life.

In order to prevent any confusion, I would like to emphasize one very essential thing – unlike creating health in your own body, which only requires your thoughts and focus on health to change the chemistry of your body, when it comes to physical wealth, which involves other people, this will not land in your lap out of nowhere; action is required. So, when you think about wealth, the universe aligns itself in such way that you stumble upon other people who will help you on your journey toward wealth, which will provide either ideas or support to help you achieve that desire; however, if no action on your part is taken with that information or in respect to that support, no reaction will be returned from the universe. Dreaming of riches will not make you rich – acting on opportunities will do. The more opportunities you seize, the closer you get to your dream.   *choosing not to – ?*

Attitude toward the little things makes all the difference we need in life. The choices we make every moment decide the outcome. A person who walks with their eyes on their phone, distracted by whatever they see on there, may shoulder you by mistake, but how you choose to react to that event makes a massive difference. You can choose to be kind, understand it was a mistake, forgive, and let go, which will elevate your vibration and bring about more positive vibrations, or you can choose to be offended by the lack of respect of that person toward you and attempt to teach them a lesson, which can only lead to negative vibrations that will start bringing about more negative events.

Choosing the attitude you adopt toward every little thing that happens in your day-to-day life sharpens your awareness and, in time, shapes your character. Your character is what decides the general frequency you put yourself on by default. If you develop kindness, your body will start to vibrate on this frequency and put you in

[Handwritten note at top: "What if you repress? Actively trying to be kind?"]

situations that will show you more kindness. If you develop anger, your body will start to vibrate on this frequency and put you in situations that will show you more anger. Either of these two, if persisted upon, will integrate in your character, whether voluntarily or involuntarily. The good thing is that it doesn't matter what path you've been on so far; you can shift your attitude toward who you want to be, and through awareness you can choose the response to most of the events in your day-to-day activity until such point that life will start presenting to you more circumstances and events that will match your choices, therefore making it so much easier to create a life by design by default.

Comparison with others is also a matter of attitude. According to your perspective, you can see a person as superior or inferior, stronger or weaker, or wealthier or poorer. There was this story I read on a few occasions on social media where a rich father took his son to a village where they spent a few days on a farm of what would be considered a very poor family to show him how poor people live. On their way back from the trip, the father asked his son how he liked the trip.

"It was great, Dad!" the son replied.

"Did you see how poor people live?" asked the father.

"Oh, yes," replied the son.

"So, what did you learn from this trip?" asked the father.

The son replied, "I learned that we only have one dog and they have four; they also have a cat, and a few chickens. We have a pool, but they have a creek that stretches for miles. They have the night's sky full of stars and we only have lanterns to light our garden. Our patio reaches the front garden and they have the whole horizon. We have only a small garden where I can play but they have fields that go beyond our sight. We have to buy our food but they get to grow theirs. We have walls and fences to protect our property but they don't need protection because they're surrounded by friends and family."

His father was speechless, and sensing that, the son continued, "Thank you for showing me how poor we are and I promise that I will be more grateful for the little we have."

The moral of this little story is that happiness never comes from the amount of things one possesses but from their attitude toward the life they live and the way they accept and use what they have. It is true that one thing may bring a different experience in one's life, but once that experience has been accomplished, the thing that helped becomes redundant. You may want to experience jumping off a plane with a parachute, if that would make you happy, but that doesn't mean you have to wait until you have enough money to buy the plane. Hypothetically, let's imagine that miraculously you have stumbled upon the kind of money that will allow you to buy a plane and you do, then you go on to jump off it with the parachute. The experience was exhilarating and you want to do it one more time, and you go again and again until you've had enough. What will happen with that plane after the experience is over? Do you think it will bring you happiness knowing it is sitting there in a hangar waiting for you? Does it bring you comfort knowing that you own something that the other 99% of the world doesn't? The experience itself makes you happy, not the possession of things.

Wearing branded clothes won't make you happy; mostly, they will make you feel superior to a specific category of people, but the quality of the clothes will bring a different experience. What's the point in wearing a T-shirt that has a brand written in big bold letters if it makes you itchy all the time? What's the point in wearing a pair of shoes that make you look pretty but they hurt your feet to the point you'd hit someone with a brick if they "stepped on your toe"? Do they make you happy? And if they don't, why do it in the first place? Oh, I think I know what it is – we see other people wearing them in ads or on the street and because we see them cocky and smiling, we assume they are happy, so we want something like that. We would love a T-shirt or a pair of shoes that will make us happy, of course we would. Who wouldn't want a cover that will make us happy? Unfortunately, happiness is an inside job;

it's a choice, not a face that you put on, not a T-shirt, nor a pair of shoes. We choose happiness by choosing to see the bright side, and by choosing to keep a positive mental attitude in spite of what life may throw at us.

> *"Some people are so poor, all they have is money."*
> *—Patrick Meagher*[2]

The things that make us wealthy are never the things we can buy with money but the things that are free – a person who can tell you, "I love you," someone who can hold you in their arms when you feel like everything around you is crumbling to pieces, or someone who can hug you when you get home. None of these can be bought with money, and without them, all the money in the world won't bring about that experience. You, with your character and with your actions, will bring about in your life the people who can show you their love and appreciation. Tell a person that you are a millionaire and then tell another person that they are the most amazing person you've met, and then see which one appreciates you more, which of them will want to spend their days with who you are, and which of them will want to spend their days with what you have.

We all are rich one way or another, but we don't always have the eyes to see it. We compare ourselves with others and attempt to be better than them, to look smarter, or highlight special features, trying to pose on a higher level, forgetting the most important thing – our own happiness.

[Margin note: Making out of survival habit?]

We are so blinded by what other people say and do that we become ashamed of who we are and no longer allow ourselves to be who we are. We put on different masks so we can fit in different places as if being part of some exclusive club will make us happy. Sorry to disappoint, but that will only bring about more reasons to pretend to be someone who you are not so you can fit someplace you don't belong.

So, how do we go about finding happiness? First off, you need to look inside yourself, probably as deep as going back to childhood and removing the multitude of layers and masks you've stacked up over time. I, for one, used to have a mask for my parents. They told me what they wanted me to be, and I pretended to be that. I had one for my friends, so I could be accepted; one for my school colleagues; one that I would pose on the street; one that I would take to a club; one to win an interview and go to work; one to woo a girl; and so on. Deep under these covers I found myself loving, smiling, selfless, open, and tolerant, with a splash of curiosity and a drive to serve others. As soon as I'd allowed this hidden gem to shine out in the open, all the masks I'd created over time became redundant. Now, I get to be myself; some people don't like me, but that's their problem, and I never stress over the opinion of others. I listen to their arguments and accept them as their own, and sometimes they may trigger some ideas in my mind that I may follow, but only if it suits me.

[Margin note: ? Expand ?]

I do have a rule – whatever I do for my happiness should never harm another human being. What I mean by this is that I will not go as far as stepping on people's toes just so it will suit my comfort. Yes, I am focusing on my own happiness, but I choose to step away from a confrontation, fight, or any situation that may cause harm to others. If I'm on a plane and the flight attendant announces that there is a person allergic to nuts, no matter how badly I crave those nuts in my bag, I hold off on them until we get off the plane. This rule also applies to the non-physical plane – I hold off on expressing my opinion about any person present or not, and that isn't because it may harm their reputation, which could be the case sometimes, but because it harms mine. You see, what we say about others is not as much about them as it is about us. We think that if we call a person names we become superior to them. Words do have power, and this power influences the person who wields the words more than the person to which they are directed.

If you don't have the time or the strength to start digging through your past and uncover that happy you, there is another option that allows you to start where you are and move from there – accept what is as it is and make peace with the reality. Let go of the resistance to control outcomes and the compulsive will to cover appearances. The situation you're in is a direct reaction to the things you did and thoughts you've had. Accept that! Own it! Learn from it and change the way you think and behave to prevent this kind of situation from happening again in the future if it makes you uncomfortable. Let's say you managed to lie your way out of the situation, but the situation hasn't changed. The next day, it'll still be there waiting for you and you'll have to keep on lying and cover it up over and over, and that brings about stress that keeps on building up until it is so heavy that you are crushed under it. Moreover, if your friends found out about it they will tease you about it because they find it funny to see you uncomfortable, though if you manage to find peace with it and accept it, you may even get comfortable telling that story yourself and laugh with them about it. Some people resort to alcohol for coping, and others resort to drugs to numb the feeling of guilt that weighs within, but the easiest and simplest way is to allow the events to run their course and accept them as they come. Suffering does not come from the things that happen but from our resistance to them and our stubbornness to change what is into something that you think others want to see.

Above all, the best way to find happiness is to focus on the things that bring you joy and that make you laugh. In the words of PT Barnum, "Laughter is the best medicine. There's nothing like laughter to sweeten life. Laughter adds a touch of sunshine to even the darkest day."[8] Laughter strengthens your immune system, boosts mood, diminishes pain, and protects you from the damaging effects of stress.

Nothing works faster or more dependably to bring your mind and body back into balance than a good laugh. It also helps you release anger and forgive easier. This priceless medicine is fun, free, and easy to use. A good, hearty laugh relieves physical tension and stress, leaving your muscles relaxed. Laughter decreases stress hormones and increases immune cells and infection-fighting antibodies, thus improving your resistance to disease. Laughter triggers the release of endorphins, the body's natural feel-good chemicals. Endorphins promote an overall sense of well-being and can even temporarily relieve pain. You can't feel anxious, angry, or sad when you're laughing. Laughter shifts perspective, allowing you to see situations in a more realistic, less threatening light. A humorous perspective creates psychological distance, which can help you avoid feeling overwhelmed and diffuse conflict. As Groucho Marx said, "I, not events, have the power to make me happy or unhappy today. I can choose which it shall be. Yesterday is dead, tomorrow hasn't arrived yet. I have just one day, today, and I'm going to be happy in it."[2]

If you don't feel like laughing all the time, that's fine; just start with a smile.

3: The Mirror Effect

As above, so below; as within, so without.
—Hermes Trismegistus[10]

Often associated with the concept of correspondence in Hermetic philosophy, which states that there is a direct relationship between the internal state of an individual and the external circumstances they experience, this idea can be traced back to the Emerald Tablet, a foundational text in Hermeticism, which contains the principle, "As above, so below; as below, so above."[10] The principle suggests that the microcosm (the individual) reflects the macrocosm (the universe), and vice versa. Essentially, it means that what happens internally in an individual's mind is reflected in their external reality.

In other words, we are equally a manifestation of our environments as the environments are a manifestation of our thoughts. Everything in your life is a manifestation of your thoughts, and yes that includes people as well. We may not have created those people, but through the magnetic power of our thoughts, we bring about those people in our lives, and yes that includes our parents and siblings. The thing is, we can only choose from the people we attract in our lives as a result of our vibrational states.

Are we to serve our parents in some way?

How to Deal With Everything

So, our frequencies match these people to us because of their specific traits that resonate with our beliefs and what we do by being who we are. In fact, we prompt them to act the way they do in our presence. Our existence in their lives makes them who they are in the same way their existence in our lives makes us who we are. We may have started as a manifestation of our parents' thoughts and actions, but through our existence in their life we influenced them to act the way they do. On this physical plane we may not be able to explain our choice to be born into a specific family, but as the law of cause and effect applies with universal precision in all other aspects of our lives, we can only conclude that we are the cause of our parents. On the quantum level we started as a speck of energy in the form of a thought, and through the law of attraction we brought about our existence into the world. When we think in terms of energy and frequency, we can no longer talk about good and bad or light and dark. All things are energy on different vibrations, different frequencies that manifest as physical. An acorn becomes an oak by changing its vibrational energy, and throughout this process it attracts the water and the nutrients required to become a tree. So, if you think you didn't choose to be born into that family of yours, think of it as a starting point in a transformational journey that has led you to become who you are right now. You wouldn't be who you are if you hadn't started where you did and been through the stages you've passed. That is what makes you unique, though we are all connected through this energy field that is the source of all physical manifestation.

The people in our lives are but mirrors that show us the things we cannot see within us. Imagine you're in a boarding school and a prank has been played on you. You wake up and everyone starts laughing and pointing their fingers at you but you can't figure out why. You look at yourself – arms, hands, chest, belly, legs, and feet on all sides you can reach with your sight – and still can't figure out anything out of the ordinary that would trigger them to laugh like that. Eventually, you go to the toilet and look in a mirror. Once you glance at your reflection, you understand why they've been laughing.

People are like that, mirrors that show us things within us that we can only see by looking at them. And our biggest mistake is in our hopeless attempt to change the people we look at so they would show us what we want. In our ignorant minds, we think that if we change the people in the mirror, or the mirror itself for that matter, we become different. We are what we see in the people around us, in those mirrors. For the people around us to change, and for that reflection to change, we have to change. We have to make a deliberate choice to change – change our thoughts, actions, and choices – and by doing so we change our vibrational states, which in turn brings about new kinds of people in our lives who will match who we are, and who will show us a new reflection of who we are.

Think about it! Homeless and jobless people are surrounded by homeless and jobless people, religious people are surrounded by religious people, and successful people are surrounded by successful people. Any of these people has the ability to choose to be different. It may seem impossible from where they are because all they can see is the same kind of people who match their frequency, and they may tell themselves there is no other way; this is what life looks like. There are plenty of homeless people who became successful because they started changing their thoughts and believed in them, which brought about people and circumstances that matched their belief and helped them become successful. Examples like this are: Jim Carey, Sylvester Stallone, Jennifer Lopez, Daniel Craig, Steve Harvey to name a few. There are also successful people who lost everything, again as a result of changing their thoughts and beliefs. **The reality you see around is a direct manifestation of the reality you see within you.**

When in a relationship, you're better off being kind than being right. We all have different opinions about things, different perspectives, but when we try to impose our visions onto the people with whom we interact, not only do we set ourselves on a fighting field, but we also put that

WRITE DOWN -
REALITY IS,
REALITY I WANT TO SEE.
REALITY I DON'T WANT TO SEE

relationship at risk of disintegrating. When you win an argument, the other party is losing, and they won't like being in a relationship where they are the loser. They want to be in a relationship where they feel supported. So, instead of starting an argument in which to prove who's right or who's best, just take a moment to understand the other party's point of view. This way, you won't allow your mind's ego to break free and sabotage your relationship; instead, if you take control and with kindness offer your companionship when they need to weigh their point of view and yours, they can reach a decision point all on their own. They will respect you more for being kind than they will for proving them wrong.

How do you deal with those stubborn people who think they're always right and don't even bother to consider your point of view? The answer to that is that you don't. You don't have to deal with them or with their point of view. The thing is, you don't have to stay in a relationship where you don't feel respected, though my argument is that they are in your life for a reason, so you may as well deal with it, learn from it, and cleanse it. When you deal with them, ==just remember that they are only talking from the limitations of their mind, from their perspective, and their point of view.== Do not take it personally. You did not attract this person in particular into your life – you've attracted the way they're acting. If you end that relationship, another person will come into your life to act the same way, and though it may seem like they're attacking you, in reality they're only harming themselves. They're only holding on to hot coal and throwing it at you, burning themselves more in the process. They're drinking poison but believing they're hurting you. It wasn't easy for me in the beginning to accept that, and my mind's Ego was kicking and shouting, but with pause and reflection, I started mastering the art of kindness. I got to the point where as soon as I felt my mind's Ego getting up, I knew the trouble was about to start and put out the fire before it spread too wildly.

Being kind requires love. In order to be kind to somebody, you must be able to love them, and to love them you have to understand they are someone special who deserves your love – like thinking they are just like you, and by loving them you are loving yourself, and by being kind to them you are being kind to yourself.

When we change the root cause of our environments – our very own thoughts – the environments start changing as well to match the new frequency of our thoughts. When we change our thoughts, our beliefs change, which causes us to change. When we change, what we see in other people changes, and what they see in us changes as well. It all starts within. It all starts with one thought over which you have 100% control. You can sit and soak in your current situation or you can start shifting your thoughts toward who you want to be. Nobody will be able to knock on your mind's door and say, "Hey, what are you doing here?" That is your very own sanctuary, the only place where you can do whatever you want, where you can paint in colorful pictures the person you want to be, the people you want to attract, and the experiences you want to live.

Whatever we see around us is but a manifestation of what is within us. The world outside is a perfect match to the world inside, a mirror that shows us in the physical plane what we can't see in our minds. Most of us get frustrated that things don't go how we expect and start blaming this and that for whatever it is that didn't work. If we'd only acknowledge the power we have to control our environments with our thoughts alone, that frustration will disappear. All stress would dissipate in the knowledge that we can change what is by changing what we are and who we are. When you look in the mirror and see that you have some dirt on your forehead, would you try to clean the mirror and get frustrated with it to the point of throwing a tantrum and breaking that mirror?

Use what you see in the mirror of your mind, the world around you that is, to wipe out the dirt in you. Trying to fix things in the physical world, to fix people and get them to change so that they can do and be what you want them to be, is laborious and very stressful work. That's what takes away our happiness. "My kids won't do that; my boss doesn't see me; my spouse doesn't listen to me; my parents won't approve of me, etc." They all go away in the realization that we created that. It's hard to swallow, I know, and it is frustrating to know that you are the cause of it all and don't know what to do to fix it, but hey! We didn't know how to walk when we came into this world, and we didn't know how to speak the language of the people around us. It took us a bit of perseverance and determination, and eventually we managed to walk, and we managed to make ourselves understood.

Don't beat yourself up over the fact that you're trying to change your thoughts and you're visualizing your ideal life but nothing seems to change, because they do change even if you can't see it right away. Every single thought you create resonates throughout the entire universe and it moves things around to match your frequency. Our physical eyes may not have the ability to see that change right away, and that's where faith comes into play. Faith is not the confirmation of the things you want; it's the ability to see and act as if they are already what you want. As you go on with your life, the world around you starts rearranging itself to match that faith, to match that belief, and to match those thoughts in your mind.

What we see is an exact replica of the thoughts we've created until now. Every cut off in traffic that made us angry, every fight we had with our spouses, and every thought of hatred we had toward our bosses have contributed to the mirror we now see around us. You will not change a thing around you if you don't acknowledge that you are responsible for what is. You will not change a thing around you if you don't acknowledge that it is within your power to do so. You will not change a thing around you if you don't change yourself.

Handwritten annotation:
Situation where changing yourself is detrimental?
Lowering stance?
Maybe.
Just be kind..

4: Love

Love is the most powerful force in the universe. When you love yourself, you can love others. When you love others, you can change the world.
—*Don Miguel Ruiz*[4]

I love, because I choose to love. My love is not dependent on the person I love. Love is my state of being. I choose to share my love because that is the life in me; it flows through my veins and it beats my heart. I am love. I choose to allow this high frequency energy to flow through me and on to the people around me. Whether the other person deserves it or not is not for my mind to judge but for my love to touch and bless.

We say sometimes that this or that person does not deserve love because they are like this or they did that. I think that those who need our love the most are exactly those who our minds think shouldn't deserve our love, because we don't love with our minds. A criminal did whatever they did because they lost their ability to love and felt compelled to show that to the world through the act they committed. That's a person empty of love and a person who deserves to be filled with our love. We think in our minds that those loving people out there are the ones who deserve our love, but the truth is we feel compelled to love them purely because their vibration demands love from those around them. They choose to be good and spread their love and, by law, in return they attract more love in their life – that is why you feel like they are deserving of your love. It's not actually your choice – you're attracted to it; you're pulled into it.

But you can't love someone if you don't love yourself first. Until you find a way to accept yourself for who you are and the way you are, you'll always find negatives in others and reasons to not accept them for who they are. Until you can go in front of a mirror and look yourself in the eyes and confidently say, "I Love You!" you'll always struggle to love other people. Fill yourself first with your own love. Love does not come in limited supply. Love is abundant and limitless, so give yourself all the love you can, then share that love everywhere you go. Smile at people, be kind to them, hug them, and give them a piece of your love and that's when you'll feel happiness.

You may not know where to start and how to love yourself, and that's ok. You can try this in the mirror – look yourself in the eye and start appreciating all your features, and then muster a feeling of gratitude. Once you feel that vibrating in your body, focus on it and bring up to the surface all the things you are grateful for about yourself, like the fact you are breathing – be grateful for that. Your heart pumps in your chest – be grateful for that. All the healthy parts of your body – be grateful for each and every one of them. Acknowledge them and make your mind aware that there is so much to love about yourself, then smile; look at your face and smile. If tears of joy haven's started flowing down your cheeks yet, keep at it. Do this on multiple occasions until a feeling of confidence and love in yourself starts settling in.

If you're that shy and can't even look at yourself in the mirror, that's fine too. Just use what you learned in the previous chapter about the mirror effect and use the people you meet throughout your day as mirrors. Take a moment to acknowledge them and accept them for who they are. If your mind doesn't like what you see and you find it hard to accept them as they are, just start a little debate and find reasons why they deserve your acceptance and appreciation. If someone cuts me off in traffic, I say, "Bless them; they must be in a hurry somewhere." If someone shows anger and they appear disturbed, I say, "Bless them; they're probably going through a rough day!" Find whatever reasons you can to accept them just the way they are and ==realize that they're in your life and in front of your eyes to help you learn to accept and love yourself.==

> *"To Love is to recognize yourself in another."*
> *—Eckhart Tolle[11]*

Giving is the expression of love. Whatever you give – a "good day," a smile, a penny, a hug, or anything else – through the act of giving you're showing your love. If you give a penny to a beggar, don't do it because they need it but because you need it. Our minds have this strange way of judging others for their situation, not realizing that by judging them it judges itself. If your mind starts doing that, stop it and say, "I don't know what this person has been through and the pain they suffer; it's not my place to judge them." And then show your acceptance toward them in any way that may be appropriate. I don't always carry cash on me, so if some beggar asks for money, I stop and ask them what they need it for. Most often they want food, so I ask them what they would like to eat and go to the nearest store and buy that for them.

> *"A man's highest happiness is found in the bestowal of benefits on those he loves; love finds its most natural and spontaneous expression in giving."* —Wallace D Wattles[12]

I often hear people getting into a new relationship and are fearful of sharing their feelings toward the other person. "What if they don't love me back?" This attitude of reciprocity goes both ways. As I mentioned previously, love does not come in limited supply. You're not wasting your love by giving it out, and you're not a fool for saying it out loud either; if anything, it shows courage and bravery. Your mind will try to justify that a relationship has to be fifty-fifty and your love has to be met in the middle or you're a fool. Truth is, in a relationship it is 100% your responsibility. If you want a relationship to work, you have to give your 100%. Don't judge what they are doing or not doing. You must never fear giving out your love.

> *"To fear love is to fear life, and those who fear life are already three parts dead."* —Bertrand Russell[13]

My love is my state of being. It is not dependent on the other person. If I love my spouse, I do so because I accept her just the way she is. I don't need her to dress a certain way, to look a certain way, and I don't need to change her so I can love her and be with her. My love is not based on the physical appearances or on the material things she's wearing. My love is not based on how she talks or acts. If one day she doesn't feel like being her usual self, I just need to find a way to accept her the way she is, because my love is unconditional. I simply love her because she is part of my life; she is my life, and by loving her just the way she is, I love myself just the way I am. By accepting her through her changes, I give myself permission to change and grow and become a better version of myself – to be free to be happy.

What is love? Yes, it is a feeling, an emotion, but what does that mean? The Latin word for emotion is *emotere*, which literally means "energy in motion." Like anything else on the face of the earth and throughout the entire universe, love is an energy, but it vibrates at a very high level. Dr David R Hawkins mapped a Chart of Consciousness[14] matching our feelings to frequencies. For ease of understanding, he assigned values to most of our feelings that range from 20 for the feeling of shame all the way to 700+ for enlightenment. In between, we have guilt at 30, fear at 100, courage at 200, acceptance at 350, and love at 500. Love is also the frequency of creation. When you are in love with an idea, you give life to it – you give it a physical shape. When you are in love with a plant, the plant grows stronger and healthier. When you share your love with other people, you raise their vibration; whether they want it or not, they just start feeling it throughout their body.

"Love is the only reality and it is not a mere sentiment. It is the ultimate truth that lies at the heart of creation." — Rabindranath Tagore.[15]

Love is a state of acceptance, appreciation, and gratitude. When we judge people, we come from a limited understanding of our minds. Within our minds we only have part of the information. It's like looking at a sphere and saying it is a circle. The side we're looking at may appear red but the other side may as well be blue. But the most common misinterpretation comes from the glasses we're wearing. Yes, we all wear glasses in the sense that our pasts and our environments define the type of lenses we're wearing and how our minds see the world. A rich person looks down on poor people, a poor person looks down on rich people, and a religious person looks down on other religions, but a loving person looks up to all people, because in our minds we only see differences, but in our hearts we all are equal. The differences between people do not come from the color of their skin, their religion, political affiliation, or the country they were born. The differences come from our perceptions, how we see things, and how we choose what to accept and what is unacceptable.

Love is patient, love is kind. It does not envy, it does not boast, it is not proud. It does not dishonour others, it is not self-seeking, it is not easily angered, it keeps no record of wrongs. Love does not delight in evil but rejoices with the truth. It always protects, always trusts, always hopes, always perseveres. Love never fails. (Saul of Tarsus, 1 Corinthians 13:4-8)[16]

By choosing love, we choose happiness, kindness, selflessness, and faith in a better world. Love your neighbors in spite of their appearances because **love is an expression of who you are, not who they are.** Love your colleagues not for their ability to help you in your job, but because of your ability to help them shine brighter, and that's what leaders do; they empower people with their love.

> *"When the power of love overcomes the love of power the world will know peace."* —*Jimi Hendrix.*[17]

Within our minds, we think our time is limited to this life on earth and sometimes greed takes over. We want more, and we want bigger, and I am not saying that's a wrong thing. We should all aim to experience life to its fullest and enjoy as many experiences we can in one life. The problem is when the goal takes no account of life. People want to have riches – many and quickly – and in their limited minds they no longer see other people but targets and opportunities; humanity loses its value in the face of selfish goals. How you leave people feeling when you're no longer present is the highest form of richness.

> *"You need power, only when you want to do something harmful; otherwise, love is enough to get everything done."* —*Charlie Chaplin*[18]

I believe we are all one, and whatever I do for myself, I do for the entire world. If I'm being loving to myself, I'm being loving to the world. If I'm being kind to the world, I'm being kind to myself. This is something that we were born with, but the society we live in made us forget it; it made us forget that we are all in this together, regardless of skin color, religion, or sexual orientation. See the world through the eyes of your spirit, and your love – the one thing that connects everything and every one of us.

5: Forgiveness

One of the simplest ways to stay happy is to let go of the things that make you sad.

Think of a person who wronged you in the past. How does that make you feel? Do you think that person feels the same? I think not, because how we feel about somebody is a manifestation of our own thoughts. If they don't think they wronged you they really have no reason to feel that way. Feeling bad for something someone else did only harms you; it only harms your state of being. It's like the Buddhist saying that anger is like holding a hot coal in your hand with the intention of throwing it at someone. Before you throw it, you're the one getting burned.[19]

On the other hand, have you ever tried getting revenge on someone? If you did, you probably also realized that it doesn't change what they did. It only makes you drop your vibration to their level. It only makes you exactly like them. If there are 1,000 criminals in the world and you kill one, there will still be 1,000 criminals, because you get to replace the one you killed. In order to have peace of mind, revenge is never the answer. Holding a grudge is not a solution either; an eye for an eye will only perpetuate the "feel bad" state, increase hate, and enhance cruelty. Think about it; if I poke your eye because you poked mine, aren't we both blind? So, other than bringing someone down to match your misery, it's not going to lift you up out of your misery. It won't make you feel any better; it will only bring about a false sense of justice.

I sometimes hear people saying, "How can I forgive them? Do you know what they did to me?" Recently, my brother told me a story (and in order to protect the identity of those involved I will change the names) where a family met for a traditional meal, and in a formal way one of them, we'll name him Sam, asked for forgiveness from the others at the table.

Sara, also a made up name, stood up and said, "I can't forgive you, I'm sorry! I've suffered for too long now." Sam, confused, asked for details, to which Sara replied, "Ten years ago …" And that's when Sara unloaded the weight that she'd carried for ten years.

Sam hurt Sara unknowingly, and she suffered for ten years because she couldn't forgive Sam. For ten years Sam lived happily, in respect to this incident, and the only person who suffered was Sara because she couldn't let go; because she held that grudge, she suffered, and it was not even a constant suffering but a growing one because with every meeting and every encounter throughout the ten years, her anger expanded and was growing inside, making her more hateful and sour, until that day when the bubble burst.

It is not the person who does the hurting who suffers the most; it's the person who the hurt was brought upon. Though, if we were to dig deep, we would find that the person who does the hurting also does it out of the hurt and lack of love within themselves. If you've been hurt in any shape or form, for as long as you hold on to that memory, that anger, you will continue to suffer and pass on this suffering to the people with whom you interact. The person who hurt you will be none the wiser, because they simply pass on a feeling that's been passed on to them. Find a way to put a stop to this transfer of hurt and forgive them. Create a story that will justify their action in such a way that you can forgive them.

I held a huge grudge towards my parents for a very long time because they didn't raise me better; they could have handled some things better and they chose not to, or at least that's the story I was telling myself. One day, I was looking back at something I had done that didn't turn out the way I'd expected, and I was trying to figure out what I did wrong so I could learn from my mistake and not repeat it again. Upon recalling the events of that day, I couldn't find a single fault in my actions, and the fact that it still didn't turn out the way I'd expected it to was still bugging me. After a little while, I learned a new piece of information that, if I had known and acted on back when the events didn't turn out as I expected, may have changed the outcome so that it was in my favor. That was the light-bulb moment when I realized that at any given time, we're doing the best we can with what we have, and with the knowledge we had gathered up to that point. Your mind can only make a decision with the information it holds in its memory at this very moment. If in two hours' time you learn something new, your mind will have new information and a different decision can be reached, or a different action can be made. My parents did the best they could at the time they raised me with the knowledge and ability they had. I judged them from a different level of understanding, not necessarily higher, but simply different. When I finally understood this, I was able to let go of my grudge. I can't say forgive, because there was nothing to forgive anymore, because they didn't wrong me.

It is only in our minds, through the stories we tell ourselves, that we believe we've been wronged. If we stick to our stories, we'll never find the courage to forgive, because in those stories we've been wronged. When we find a reasonable explanation for their action, and when we change the narrative of the story and give them the benefit of the doubt and imagine they did the best they could with what they had, we will realize there is nothing to forgive, that we are all humans in a constant learning process. Change the narrative of the story and move on. You'll only have more time to enjoy life, to feel good, and live fully when you forgive and forget the "wrongdoings" of others. It's nothing personal; at the end of the day it's a manifestation of their own character, not yours. And as Don Miguel Ruiz underlined as the second agreement in his book *The Four Agreements*, "Don't take anything personally. [...] It's not about you."

In your search for happiness, anger, grudges and frustrations have no place in your heart, because as long as you hold on to these heavy loads, you will struggle to keep on going and eventually you'll give up on searching for happiness, thinking that it's just a utopian idea and you're better off sticking to what you know – your own struggles. Think of them as boulders that you have to carry with you. If you're strong enough, you may be able to drag them for a while, but eventually they'll wear you down. Let go of them, let go of that dead weight, and leave them behind you and make your journey lighter. Once you do so, you'll be able to see the possibilities that you have, the experiences that you can enjoy, and the freedom to choose them all. Forgive, forget, and move on because that's where happiness is.

You cannot control other people's actions, but you can control how you react to those actions. You cannot control people's opinions of yourself, but you can choose not to let that affect your self-confidence and self-worth. You cannot control how people act toward you and treat you, but you can control how you respond to their actions and what it means to you. You cannot control people's beliefs that may contradict your own beliefs, but you can respect their position as being theirs, and not need them to agree with you to feel secure with your own beliefs. You cannot control how other people live their lives, but you can have compassion for them and become a role model by evolving into the best version of yourself. You cannot control how people act toward each other, their violence and hatred. What you can control is your decision to forgive and love them. No matter what people are doing, You always have it within your power to accept them just the way they are. You do not have to like it. You do not have to condone it. You only need to accept that they are who they are and that you have no power to change them – you only have the power to change yourself.

6: The Golden Rule

The noblest art is that of making others happy.
—PT Barnum[20]

The Golden Rule is based on the principle that treating others as you would like to be treated yourself is the secret to a harmonious life. This principle appears in various forms in many religious and philosophical traditions and is considered a fundamental ethical guideline for interpersonal behavior. The essence of the Golden Rule is empathy and reciprocity, encouraging us to consider the feelings, needs, and perspectives of others in our actions and interactions. It is often considered a universal ethical principle because it transcends multiple religious and cultural contexts. It emphasizes a basic sense of empathy and fairness that is applicable to all human interactions.

While the Golden Rule is commonly associated with Christianity: "Do unto others as you would have them do unto you." (Matthew 7:12)[21], similar teachings can be found in many other religious and philosophical traditions.

In Judaism: "What is hateful to you, do not do to your fellow." (Talmud, Shabbat 31a)[22]

In Islam: "None of you [truly] believes until he wishes for his brother what he wishes for himself." (Hadith 13, 40 Hadith an-Nawawi)[23]

In Confucianism: "Do not do to others what you do not want done to yourself." (Analects 12:2)[24]

In Buddhism: "Hurt not others in ways that you yourself would find hurtful." (Udanavarga 5:18)[25]

On a quantum level, everything is energy. The physical world as we see it is energy materialized. The mountains are a form of energy, the waters are a form of energy, we are a form of energy, our thoughts are a form of energy, and our feelings are a form of energy. Under the microscope, everything is a form of vibration at different levels. And according to the law of cause and effect, everything is connected through this energy field. Every action has a reaction; everything we do, think, and feel triggers a response from the quantum field in the form of an energy that matches the vibration we are on in the physical plane, here in this reality.

As we are causality beings, we are the root of all effects that we see around us. You see a house – that was caused by the thoughts of a human being. They've created this image on the screen of their mind and then materialized it. A plane was first a dream in the mind of an individual; a book started as an idea in the mind of its author; a pen, a car, and a dress were all ideas – even a tree. I remember when I was a kid and I was eating cherries by the window of my parents' apartment, and as I was putting the stones on the side, a thought crossed my mind: *How amazing would it be if one of these stones could become a cherry tree?* I grabbed one of the stones and threw it by the fence in the garden. No hole dug, no watering, and nothing else, just the thought in my mind that a stone could become a cherry tree. Today, there is a cherry tree in that very spot where the stone landed that stands witness to my creative thought. Oh, and if you're wondering, no, I don't have superpowers; no more than you do anyway. The very same creative energy that flows through me also flows through you and everyone around us.

When interacting with others, our thoughts are a wave of energy that connect us – a channel of communication. When our thoughts materialize in words and actions, they are propelled onto the people with whom we interact, creating a visible interaction. However, at the energy level this connection/communication is created regardless of whether we choose to materialize it in words and actions. We, as humans, communicate at an energy level through our feelings – that gut feeling, that sixth sense. We feel the energy we intercept from others in our own bodies, whether it's the love we receive that makes our bodies vibrate to a frequency of pleasure, or the fear we sense in others that makes us guard ourselves, we intercept the energy of other people before they have the chance of saying or doing anything.

Our energy is passed on to every individual with whom we are in contact with. Whether we feel loving or angry, sad or happy, hateful or forgiving, or any other feeling for that matter, we create this wave of energy which vibrates at the level of that feeling through anybody who is around us. This energy has its source in our thoughts. What we think triggers our bodies to vibrate to the level of our thoughts. We think happy thoughts, and our bodies vibrate happily and propel a wave of high/happy energy. We think angry thoughts, and our bodies vibrate angrily and propel a wave of low/angry energy. I'm sure that you can think of at least one time when you felt someone's energy, which either made your body feel calm and at ease, or heavy and tense.

As we discussed in chapter three, we are magic mirrors for other people, and vice versa. We see in others what is within ourselves, and they see in us something that is within them. So when someone is angry with you, it's only because of what they see of themselves in you. It's not about what you did; it's what they saw in you of themselves. People are so angry with themselves that they don't even know how to deal with that anger, like a toddler throwing a tantrum in a supermarket, and they take it out on someone else.

When you judge someone, you're not doing it because of what they did but because of what you see through the filter of your perception that they did or didn't do. Your mind's perception of reality dictates that they should act in a specific way, and when they act differently or don't act at all, your mind kicks off because their action or inaction is not in alignment with your mind's expectation, which is stored as "normal." By default, it classes that act as "wrong" or out of place, and not in accordance to its expectation, and it judges it.

For a very long time, I had my hair cut short, and every person that knew me stored an image of me with that haircut which they've seen for a very long time, and their mind accepted it as it was. For a few months I failed to go to the barber, and my hair, as you can expect, grew longer. Every person that I met after a while started noticing that I'd changed and pointed out my hair. Moreover, some of them started suggesting that I needed to get a haircut. Their minds were so uncomfortable with the image they were seeing that they couldn't help but suggest I should go back to the old haircut that they've been used to for so long. So it's not about what a person does but what we expect of them to be.

When you look in that magic mirror of a person, you see what you expect to see; you see what in your mind is normal, accepted, and approved as the standard by which they are to act and behave. It is the projection of your mindset. Whether you see what you expect, or you see what is out of the ordinary, it is only through the filter of your perception that you are able to see the good, the bad, the wrong, the genius, or whatever you think you see in front of you. It is that part of yourself you see in them to which you react. Imagine now that I meet a new individual, a person that sees me for the first time with long hair. For them that's the norm, that is their image they have printed on the screen of their mind about me. If I were to go back to the haircut I had before I met this new individual, the other people who knew me before would accept this image as "back to normal"; however, for the new acquaintance, this would trigger an interjection like "Oh, you cut your hair!"

I was born in Romania and lived there for the first twenty-seven years of my life. The people who surrounded me, their traditions, rules, common sense, grew to be my norm. Whatever my mind saw was accepted as that. Not as good or as bad, but just what it was. When I moved to the UK, I moved into a new world, with people who have different traditions, rules and common sense as norm. My mind was kicking out at every corner because nothing that happened around me was any longer familiar. Along the way I visited other countries as well, and with every new world I was entering, I discovered new traditions amongst people, new rules, and common sense that for them was their norm, their standard, but for my mind everything was out of place. It was only when I started embracing the fact that people are different through the nature of their upbringing, that I was able to shift from judging to admiration and awe at the diversity that surrounds me. When I look at someone today I see a summary of their history, and their actions are but an extension of that history.

We only judge from the perspectives of our minds, of the environment it observed and accepted as norm up until that point. We don't see people for who they are, we see them for who we are, what we've become in the process. I use this as a trigger to remind myself whenever I get annoyed at people, that I only see in them what I am, so before my thoughts have the chance to trigger feelings of anger as a reaction to that event, I start chanting in my head the ho'oponopono cleansing formula, "I love you, I'm sorry, Please forgive me, Thank you!" (I'll go in more detail about ho'oponopono in the next chapter.)

Realizing that we can be in control of not only our actions but also in control of our environments is a huge step to adjusting our lives. By choosing our thoughts, we choose the energy that makes our bodies vibrate, the feelings that we feel and communicate to others. Understanding that what we see in others is also within us should only encourage us to find the empathy to forgive and love ourselves and through this self-love to vibrate the same energy toward our mirrors. When you look into that "magic mirror" that is in front of you, that's when you choose to act, and the way you act is reflected both on the mirror and on yourself as well.

I now know that everything I say or do to another human being, I say and do to myself. They are showing me who I am and I choose, whenever I can control that, to be kind, because being kind to them, I am kind to myself. I choose to learn from the people with whom I interact more about myself, something that I normally don't see in myself, and my future actions must reflect that learning.

The other day I was having a chat with somebody and he was talking on and on about something I didn't understand, which I believe made more sense in his head than he managed to express in words. It was so frustrating listening to him that I wanted so badly to interrupt him and tell him either that I got it, or to change the subject altogether. But then I remembered that he is just another magic mirror showing me a part of myself. Probably I am like that sometimes, and I would feel bad if someone interrupted me while I was trying to find my words and express how I felt, or the message I wanted to pass on. So I chose to act in kindness instead, which led me to be more of a proactive listener, and instead of shutting him down I started asking questions that helped me better understand what he was talking about.

==What we do is a manifestation of our characters.== Yes, people can be annoying and they can frustrate us, but that's only because of what we see of ourselves in them. How we react reflects the level of our growth. And I know that we can't always control how we react because we are so overwhelmed in the heat of the moment by the emotions that take control of our actions, but we can train our minds to choose a response. We can train our minds to pause and think before responding to that particular situation. By choosing the way to respond, we reshape the way we react. If we fail to choose the way we respond, that's ok; we can always look back, observe the situation, and think of how we could have dealt with that situation better. There are studies showing that what happens in our minds has the same impact as the practice you would have done in a real life experience. So, looking back and reflecting over that event and choosing in your mind a better response is like you would have done it then and there; neural pathways are created in your brain and next time you'll get better.

Choose to pause for a few seconds every time you have to respond to a situation until it becomes a habit, and that will embed in your mind's programming to the point that your reaction will be to pause and think before acting. In those moments of pausing, our minds have time to think, and we have time to choose to be kind, loving, and understanding. After all, everything we do to others we do to ourselves, and we truly deserve those few moments of pause before acting.

The Golden Rule goes beyond what we see with our physical eyes and feel with our sensory perceptions. The Golden Rule is rooted in the metaphysical laws of the universe as the essence of creation. It all starts with the thought. Your thought is seen on the screen of your mind as an image, but that thought also triggers a vibration in the universe – a signal similar to the one used in your mobile phone. When you call a friend, you have to type in a sequence of digits that are associated with the frequency on which your friend's phone is registered. Your friend's phone has a unique frequency and can only be reached by aligning your phone to the same frequency by typing in that particular sequence of numbers. If you mix some of the digits up, you reach someone else's phone frequency. Similarly, everything in the universe has a frequency that can be reached by aligning our minds to it using our thoughts, so by thinking, we align ourselves to the frequency of what we have thought, and by doing so we start seeing what is on that frequency in the physical world.

If, due to past experiences, we choose to say that people are mean, by thought alone we align ourselves with people on that frequency. It's like we're calling them on their frequency and they answer. They start appearing in our day-to-day lives, and they're going to keep on appearing for as long as we're going to call them. The more people like that you'll see, the more you will think of people like that, and by thinking, you will call even more people like that.

To stop this spiraling, all we have to do is to go back to the pause and think habit. This angry person appeared in my life because they are a magic mirror showing me a part of myself – what I have thought in the past. Now, I am going to assume that they have reasons for being like that, and I choose to see that they are also a good person. If I am a good person, surely there is some good in them as well, so I choose to treat them as a good person. This triggers thoughts of good people, which naturally will start calling on the frequency of good people, and when the good people start appearing in your life, you'll start thinking, *Ooh, what a nice person*, which calls for more nice people in your life.

Some of the mean people will still show up even after the "good and nice spiral" has started due to your past calls/thoughts, but with the newly created habit of pause and think, you will cut them some slack and transform them into the kind of people you want to see more of in your life.

In the end, if you want to be happy, always expect nothing from others. It's not that it's a bad thing to expect anything at all, but it's just that when we put our hopes on an outcome that comes from others, we have more chances to be disappointed both because we built up to it and because we feel hopeless; we're probably more frustrated with ourselves for believing that others can make us happy. I understand we can't always do everything the way we want it done, and my argument is that we should learn to accept things just as they are and just the way they come. So, if someone offers to do something for you, or you need them to do it because you have no time for it in your schedule, let them do it with no expectations of the results and allow yourself to be surprised. For me, this was a very hard thing to do as I've been a micromanager for so long, but once I started accepting things the way they came and allowed others to do things their way, I must say that I was not only impressed by their work but also by the way they did it, and in this way I learned that there is more than one way to achieve a result, and sometimes it is even faster and better.

Be kind to others. Be kind to yourself.

7: Tools to Use When Dealing With Everything

Affirmations

I hear people saying that "Affirmations are stupid and useless as nothing ever changes unless ..." And here they list all sorts of reasons. The thing is, on a daily basis we make affirmations unconsciously anyway: I am an engineer, I am a driver, I am black, I am Hispanic, I make lots of money, I can't find a job, I love my spouse, I hate this traffic, I love a glass of wine, I love the sunshine, I am frustrated, I hate this job, I grow tomatoes in my garden, nobody buys from me, and so on.

Affirmations are the foundation for beliefs. Everything we believe now started once as an affirmation. Some of these affirmations only needed one or two statements, and others needed more repetitions before they became a belief. In order to express our beliefs we also use an affirmation as exemplified above. ==Affirmations are the direct cause of our beliefs;== they create them and they are the vocal manifestation of our beliefs.

[handwritten: Breakdown: start basic + build.]

And if you are wondering what belief has got to do with anything, please allow me to explain. Beliefs are the little programs of our minds that control our everyday lives. If you think of our minds as software, beliefs are the codes that define the basis of that software and help it run. Our minds can never work against a belief because it wouldn't make sense, but You, the infinite super-powerful being that lives in your body and controls your mind, can influence the world around you by overriding your beliefs.

Think of something you would never do or something you would never eat in normal circumstances because you have a belief that forbids you from doing that, whether it is a moral belief, religious, or any other reason. Now put yourself in an extreme situation, like if your life depends on it. Your mind will keep on saying that you wouldn't break that belief no matter what, but You know better because you know You have a choice; You have the ultimate decision. You know that You have the power to break that belief in order to save your life. Your mind may say it's shameful and dishonorable, but that's just because that programming, that belief you're about to override, is the very core of your mind's functioning. Our minds, on their own, cannot work in chaos not knowing what's going to happen next; they need to be able to predict outcomes, and they need rules, and they will do all they can to enforce them, because only this way they can feel safe.

More often than we care to admit, these beliefs keep us chained to a certain lifestyle, whether that's poverty, poor health, or unhappiness, and our minds can't see a different outcome that will keep us "safe" in that comfort zone because it's the only way they can predict an outcome, and it brings about thoughts like *It's always been like this and it worked just fine! So what if we're unhappy, we're supposed to suffer so we can inherit forever happiness in the afterlife.*

I don't want to break your faith in any way, but you've received that faith through the medium of your peers, family, and society. That faith you hold so dear was seeded in your mind through repetitive affirmations by those around you from the moment of your first breath to the point that you never thought you had a say in it. Ever since, you've lived a life programmed for you by those very beliefs. Those beliefs may have been suitable for those people who passed them on to you at the time of their living, but you live in a different time, and you are experiencing an evolved life that, funnily enough, was made possible by the very people who implanted those beliefs into your mind. Those beliefs were good and were suitable to evolve the times they lived in. You live now in a new era, one that needs new beliefs – a set of beliefs that will guide YOU to the destination of Your choice. Instead of blindly following some old traditions because "It's always been like this," try and think for yourself for once and do what makes YOU happy and what makes YOU feel good, because this is Your life and Your experience, and YOU get to choose how you live it.

I don't want to make this book a petition against your religion, your faith, or your lifestyle, but the sad thing is that not even those who established these beliefs into our minds always know why they believe what they preach. They, too, probably follow some ageless rules they don't understand, similarly to the experiment we spoke about in the first chapter. As a child I loved going to church; in fact, I loved it so much that when faced with a limited number of choices to pursue in my studies, I chose theology. Being in a revered school that deals with both the visible world as much as it does with the invisible one, I was curious to understand why some of things were the way they were, and sadly enough, the most common response to my questions was "Believe and do not doubt." The teachers, who were preparing us to become the new priests of the church, didn't have the answers to the simple questions of a child's mind. They probably never realized they were following a belief they didn't understand, and if they did, they never had the courage to question it. Driven by the ego of their minds, they would rather shut us down with "Believe and do not doubt" than look into the question, most probably fearful of the answer they would find and realize that their life might have been built on an illusion.

==Our lives are controlled by our beliefs to a very high degree, but most of these beliefs are not ours to start with, so we end up living a life programmed for us by others,== and there is no doubt that everything they wanted for us

identify find which skill resonate + those that create conflict.

had their best interests at heart. It was their belief they passed on to us because they believed it to be "the way." But that is the very reason for our unhappiness. We follow some programming that doesn't seem to ever align with our desires, and we force ourselves with further arguments/affirmations why we should keep on following those beliefs.

But the same way we enforce those beliefs in our lifestyles, we can introduce new beliefs. Whatever you feel that is holding you back from your happiness, your health, and your overall well-being, it can be changed through affirmations. You can reprogram your mind; You can introduce new beliefs that align with what makes you happy. It won't happen with one affirmation, and that's a good thing because our minds are not that fragile, and once we embed a new belief, we can rest assured that it won't easily go away and will serve our happiness for many years to come.

When creating an affirmation, we have to be mindful of two things – our minds work in pictures, and they don't recognize negation. For instance, if I say to you, "Don't think of a giraffe!" a picture of a giraffe would have already appeared on the screen of your mind, so when saying an affirmation, we have to focus on what we want, not on what we don't want. It also needs to be stated in the present tense as if it is a fact. Your mind accepts what you feed it if it thinks it's a new piece of information that is true right now, in this very moment. So, if you're not happy with the shape of your body, you'll have to introduce a belief that will match the image of the body that will make you happy, and an affirmation for this could be "I am so happy and grateful now that **I have** this amazing body." Bear in mind that if you want to lose weight, the affirmation cannot be "I'm so happy and grateful now that I have lost so much fat," because when you say "fat," the image of a fat person appears on the screen of your mind, and you don't want that, do you? So choose the words that will bring images of the person that you want to be onto the screen of your mind, so you'll need to think "slim" instead – "I am so happy and grateful now that I have a slim body."

If you're not happy with your health, pick affirmations that will reinforce a strong and healthy body – "I am so happy and grateful now that I have a strong and healthy body!" "I am so happy and grateful now that health flows through my veins," or "I am so happy and grateful now that my body is healing at a faster than normal rate."

Here's how you can create a very powerful, personalized list of affirmations that will actually work because they resonate with you. Take a moment to look into your life at all the negative things. Yes! Negative things! Not the good ones, but the bad ones – those that make you feel bad.

These are the things you want to change in your life if your goal is to find happiness, and you can't change them if you don't know which ones they are. Get a pen and a sheet of paper and write down:

What are the things that make you feel bad?

What are the bad feelings you have about yourself?

What do you hate about yourself?

What do you hate about other people?

What negatives happen in your life on a continuous basis that make you feel bad?

What makes you sad?

What makes you angry?

How does that feel? Terrible? Great! These are the things that affect your energy, mood, and wellbeing. It's no use in saying affirmations that don't resonate with you; they'll be empty words. On the other hand, these are the things that drag you down and you must change. This is the weight that pulls you down and needs to be changed into a hot-air balloon that lifts you up.

For the next part of the exercise, take another sheet of paper and write down the following two questions: "What do I like about myself?" and "What are the qualities that I really love about myself?" Then write down as many possible things that you really love about yourself; You have to write down at least the same number of good things as the bad things you listed above. I know there is good in you, even though you may not be able to see it yet. If you get stuck, read these two questions again and again until you find a number of good things that, at least, equal the number of bad things. Each one of them should be positive, in the present tense, and start with "I Am." The power of these two words is unbelievable!

Now we have a list of negatives and a list of positive affirmations. The next part of the exercise is to change the negatives into positive affirmations. So, continuing on the list of positive affirmations, take each negative, find its opposite word, and create a positive affirmation. For instance, if you wrote "I am broke," write down "I am wealthy" or "I am rich." If you wrote "People make me sad," your affirmation should be "People make me happy." "I have no friends" will become "I have more than enough friends." "People hate me" will become "I am loved," and so on.

The positive things we wrote down already have the trust of our minds. You know they are true, and when you say them, their power lifts up your energy and your vibration. On this higher level of energy, we can now apply the new affirmations on the same vibration – the feel good vibration – and this way we give power to the new affirmations.

Take a moment and read the whole list of affirmations.

How does that feel? Now try to add some passion; read them out loud if it helps and do it five times in a row.

Well? Can you feel the power of your affirmations? This is the best list you can use because it matches your very own situation. It's tailored to you – to change your negative thoughts into positive. You see, it's not the repetition of some positive words that makes us feel better; it's the feeling that springs inside when we say these words and the energy associated with them that have the power to change our state of being.

Write them down on a card and carry them with you everywhere, and whenever you feel down, take the card out and read these affirmations a few times in a row. Read them when you wake up to get a boost of positiveness, and read them before you go to sleep so you will have sweet dreams. Keep in mind that every so often you will transform into a different person. The more you say these affirmations, the higher your level of vibration is going to be, so my suggestion is to take some time once in a while and write down again what you think is negative and what's good about yourself. You will notice that some of the things you hate right now will show on your loved list.

Remember that your current situation is the result of your beliefs. Let's call them unconscious beliefs. These beliefs created who you are right now. Changing these beliefs will change who you are, but they could also be stubborn and resistant to being replaced, so You have to be persistent. To make the affirmations stronger, add a voice to them – say them out loud, shout them if you can, and feel your chest vibrating when you say them because all that energy helps change your beliefs at a superfast pace. If you're driving alone in the car to or from work, shout your affirmations.

With every opportunity you have, repeat them over and over. As a delivery driver, while waiting by the door for the customer to answer, I would repeat all sorts of affirmations. If I have to wait in a queue somewhere, I will repeat affirmations, because I know that changing my beliefs will ultimately change my life and I use every opportunity to work on shaping what controls most of my life.

In my morning routine, I've got this A4 notebook where I jot down my affirmations. I basically keep writing until the whole page is filled with positive vibes. It might sound simple, but putting those affirmations on paper has a real kick to it. Writing affirmations is like a secret weapon for boosting focus and making those positive beliefs stick in your mind. Plus, it's a mindful moment; you're right there with your thoughts, doing the affirmations dance. And guess what? It also nudges you into some self-reflection. And here's the cool part – writing them down isn't just about the words. It's like a whole sensory experience. You're visually crafting letters into words on paper, and it's like you're painting your affirmations in your mind. It's not just a mental thing; it's a full-body, hands-on, real-deal experience. You've got the tactile vibe too – feeling the pen, moving your hand. It's like your body's absorbing those affirmations. It makes them feel more legit, like you can touch and hold on to those positive thoughts. Oh, and get this, writing has this memory-boosting superpower. You're not just writing stuff; you're engraving it into your memory. That means those affirmations will stick in your subconscious for a very long time.

Education

This has been the tool that, for centuries, has lifted up people all over the world. Now what do you think education means? Because I'm not talking about the schooling system where you go as a child and two decades later you get out of it with accumulated knowledge and a diploma to prove what information you have stored in your mind. That may be called education, but it's not what I have in mind. The way I see it, if that kind of education lifted people up, the teachers and professors would be the leaders of the world because they have the highest amount of information and knowledge. If that kind of knowledge made people happy, they would be the happiest people around. If that kind of information made people rich, they would be the wealthiest people we know.

Education, from my point of view, is the process of continuous learning. I agree that the schooling system provides the basic information, but that's just it – basic information which you can find in any library. It is true that it enhances your mind's ability to expand and creates stronger neural pathways in your brain that help you better process the information, or as Emerson put it, "The mind, once stretched by a new idea, never returns to its original dimension,"[26] but that's not enough.

I believe that education is something that should come as a necessity for becoming the best version of yourself. The term "education" is derived from the Latin words *educare*, meaning "to bring up," and *educere*, meaning "to bring forth."[27] If you want to be a musician, you will study and educate yourself in that field with the goal of being the best you can be in that field. Practicing and learning new techniques is what makes you educated. If you stop educating yourself, you stagnate. If you want to be a medical doctor, you don't stop learning when you get your diploma and your practice. You keep on educating yourself to find new ways to help your patients.

I, for one, learn every day. I keep on reading and listening to books to constantly better myself, and to become a better human in the support of my fellow humans. Thinking that learning ends once you get a diploma is naive. Life gives unique challenges to each and every one of us, and our abilities to overcome these challenges is determined by our will to do it and our preparedness. Zig Ziglar said, "Success occurs when opportunity meets preparation."[28] Though I believe he took Seneca's saying, "Luck is what happens when preparation meets opportunity"[29] and adapted it; I think they both have the same goal – to point out that preparedness mixed with opportunity are the keys to progress.

Decide your end goal in life – what you want to do and who you want to be – and study everything you can get your hands on that helps you on that path. The more you study, the better you will get and the more valuable you will become, because what you gather in your mind is a fortune that nobody can take away from you. And when the opportunity arises, you'll be ready to take action, not because you've learned what you needed but because you are willing to learn more and more – you are becoming curious and eager to discover more.

The key to improving always begins with yourself. It starts with the humble acceptance that no one really has knowledge, and to gain knowledge you have to admit you have no knowledge. To be humble in our possession of knowledge is to be open to education, while to be proud of our knowledge is to become closed off to new information. When we realize that we know very little compared to what we can learn, an awareness of our ignorance arises and it motivates us to find out more. An acknowledgment of someone's own lack of knowledge forces them to look elsewhere to acquire that knowledge. The moment you think that you have all the answers, you have no incentive to discover more. On the other hand, to admit you are ignorant, or at least lacking in knowledge, is a motivational blessing. With this mindset, you are open to new ideas, opportunities, and possibilities.

Humility is part of this process of education. This is also because we have to admit we can also find knowledge in and through other people. It can be a blow to the ego to concede that others know something that we do not, but when we seek the advice of many, it becomes apparent that we are not dependent on just one or two people. The goal is to take information from many different sources, and then extract, simplify, and combine it into knowledge. To get there, you must first admit that you do not possess all the answers, but that together with others, you can come to an adequate grasp of the whole.

Though in the age of technology, knowledge is still not something that you can acquire at the click of a mouse or tap of a phone – you have to go after it. This active process called education always begins with you, but it never really ends. It gives you the drive to be curious, to search the World Wide Web, to read the next book, and to constantly ask questions of the people who you meet. It transforms you into a good listener, it makes you patient and humble, and it makes you a better human being overall and resilient in your search for happiness.

Exercise

Physical exercise is by far one of the most important tools that you can use to achieve a state of happiness. It enhances your mood, reduces stress, and improves sleep. Physical activity stimulates the production of endorphins – the body's natural mood elevators – which can lead to a feeling of euphoria known as the "runner's high." It also reduces stress hormones like cortisol and adrenaline, helping to alleviate anxiety and improve overall stress management. Additionally, regular exercise can regulate sleep patterns, leading to deeper and more restful sleep, which in turn reduces symptoms of depression and anxiety.

Exercise boosts cognitive function and brain health by promoting the growth of new brain cells and enhancing memory, attention, and processing speed. It helps regulate neurotransmitters such as dopamine and serotonin, which are crucial for mood regulation. Regular physical activity has been shown to be as effective as antidepressant medications for some individuals, offering a natural way to alleviate symptoms of depression and anxiety. This cognitive boost also extends to better emotional regulation and resilience to stress. Beyond physiological benefits, exercise also enhances self-esteem and social interaction. Improved physical fitness can lead to a better body image and increased self-confidence.

You don't have to aim for the Olympics, though that wouldn't be such a far-fetched idea – you only have to aim for a habit. It doesn't matter how small you start; what matters the most is consistency. Setting up a time in the day to exercise and doing it regularly is the key to a healthier and happier life overall. In the beginning, you may not be able to run a marathon or lift 200 lb, and that's absolutely fine, but being consistent will get you there. Small steps will get you even further than you can ever imagine. When I started high school, I was not even able to do three push-ups, but I decided in my mind that every day I would do one more than the previous day. The next day, I pushed myself to do the third push up. The following day, I knew I could do the three and pushed myself to do the forth. The day after that, I knew I could do four and pushed myself to do the fifth, and so on, until eventually I was doing over fifty push-ups in one go.

What we believe we can do becomes really easy to do, and when we add just a little more, we stretch that belief that we can do a little bit more. If I had jumped from three push-ups to six the next day, I would have scared my mind into guarding itself and raise a wall of doubts and reasons why I couldn't double my performance. Guiding it in little steps, I helped it expand its comfort zone. So, start as small as you can and keep at it every day, and consistency will build habit, habit will build confidence, and confidence will empower you to reach higher.

Gratitude

This is a tool that helps us shape both our minds and our environments. When we are being grateful, our bodies start releasing dopamine and serotonin, the feel good chemicals that help the mind produce more positive thoughts and help the body with increased positive emotions. It enhances our moods and helps us create stronger interpersonal relationships. It strengthens our immune systems and improves our sleep-wake cycles. Being grateful makes us healthier and happier.

I don't want you to **think** that if you catch a cold and say, "Thank you for my health," you'll be miraculously healed. But if you condition your mind that you have full control over your body and get to the point where you truly **believe** it, a miracle **is** possible and you will be able to aid the healing of your body by simply saying, "Thank you for my health." Our bodies are completely susceptible to our thoughts and beliefs. Our brains will act directly under the impressions that our minds make on it. You have the power to change the structure of your body in accordance with your belief. If you believe you have a weak body and can catch a cold easily, at the first sneeze you hear in the same room, you'll very shortly start getting symptoms of a cold. But if you believe you have a strong immune system that can fight any disease, your body will act in accordance with your belief.

Building that kind of belief doesn't happen overnight, though. Along with a set of affirmations repeated whenever your mind is free, a deep sense of gratitude and focus on what you do want to see in your life – to manifest – is necessary. The energy of gratitude vibrates throughout your body and throughout the whole universe. It calls for more of the things you are grateful for to come and meet you on that frequency you raise yourself on.

As soon as I wake up, before getting off the bed I start expressing gratitude for all the things that I have and want to have in my life as if I already have them. I also do this throughout my day. One of the things that is always present in my gratitude list is my health – "I'm so happy and grateful that I have a strong and healthy body. I'm so happy and grateful that health is flowing through my body.

Thank you! Thank you! Thank you!" This statement that I reinforce in my mind every morning created the belief that my body is strong and healthy and can heal very fast.

One day, as I was doing deliveries as a courier, I caught my finger in the side door of the van as it was shutting. I had to drop the parcels from my other hand on the ground so I could open the door again to pull my fingers out. I didn't realize how bad it was until I got to the customer's door and whilst waiting for them to open the door I saw a pool of blood at my feet dripping from my finger. I started chanting, "Thank you for my health; thank you for my healing." Nobody opened the door at that time, so I headed back to the van to grab the first aid kit. By the time I got to the van, the flow of blood had completely stopped.

Another time, the back door of my van was open as I was searching for a parcel. A sudden gust of wind slammed the door against my head so badly that I got dizzy and lost balance. Almost as an instinct I said, "Thank you for my health; thank you for my healing." In a matter of seconds I had completely recovered and I felt like nothing had ever happened – no bump on my head, no hurt, and no pain.

But gratitude does more than just change the metabolism in the body. It also changes our perspectives toward the outside world. When we are being grateful for the good we see in other people, we shift the focus of our minds toward what we admire and love in them. This way we start seeing more good in the people around us. When we see the good in people, we treat them accordingly. People feel treated positively and react positively.

Imagine that someone has cut you off in traffic. Instinctively, you could shout from the safety of your iron box and cuss them. Then what? You're still angry and still frustrated. You could try to teach them a lesson, make a slalom through the traffic, catch them up, and cut them off as well to show them how it is. I'm sure that would make you feel a little bit better, but then how are you any different from them? How many other people would you have cut off as well to reach your goal? How many times would you expose yourself to accidents in this pursuit? And if all those people you'd cut off in your pursuit started doing the same, then what? Anger is like a hot potato that gets passed on from one person to another. Everyone gets burned until one stops passing it on.

What if, instead of responding with anger, we respond with gratitude? People have a myriad of reasons for their actions, of which we, as outsiders, have no understanding. Someone may have an emergency, or another may be late for an interview; it makes no difference either way. Our responses to their reaction decide who WE are and the kind of chain reaction we trigger. Even though, instinctively, I get overwhelmed by emotion and my mind may want to retaliate, I pause and say, "Thank You! Thank you for being safe! Thank you for having plenty of time to reach my destination! Thank you for their safe arrival to their destination! I'm sure they have a good reason for what they do, so bless them on their journey." What's the worst that can happen in this situation? What's the worst thing that can happen to a grateful person?

When we change our perspectives about the things we see with our physical eyes, we control our responses and no longer allow our instinctual reactions to control us, or to control our lives. We take charge of the near future, because we choose the next course of action. Our minds work with the limited information they gather with the physical senses, but they cannot see other people's experiences, what the catalyst of their reaction was, and what they've been through before they got where we met them. With this limited information, our minds decide who that person is. The way I see it, for a person to react in a bad way, they must have been through a tough experience, and what they need the most is not someone piling on to their already messed up day but someone to show them love and kindness. If you can't do that, a simple step back out of their way does more good to you and to them then a retaliation.

On the quantum level, as mentioned previously, we have the law of cause and effect. This law states that whatever we send into the Universe must come back. Action and reaction are equal and opposite. Everything in the entire universe happens according to this law, and there is no such thing as chance. Every effect must have a cause, and in turn, every cause must have an effect. Therefore, we have a perpetual cycle of cause and effect. If you are interested in the effects in your life, you must focus on the cause. If you want to change the effect – what you experience – you must change the cause – your thoughts and actions – and the effect will automatically take care of itself. Say good things to everyone, treat everyone with respect, and be grateful for all the good that is already filling your life, and all this will start to multiply. That is how the law works.

When we start giving thanks, we create a cause – a chain reaction for an effect that is to come back. The energy we focus on takes us to the frequency of that energy where we are bound to encounter similar frequency events. If we start cussing, we focus on that energy and we lower our beings to a frequency that is filled with similar events, which will lead us to more cussing. If, on the other hand, we start being grateful, we raise our vibrations to a frequency where we are bound to encounter more events that will show us more reasons to be grateful.

Up to a point, we are a product of our environments. We observe our surroundings, we focus on them, and in return we get to see the same thing. It is only by deliberate choice – when we choose to focus on something else in spite of what we see in our environments – that we cause the change in the environment. Imagine this – you go to work and at the end of the week/month you get a pay stub. You look at the stub, give it your focus/energy, and the next week/month you get the same stub. Now, if you start shifting your focus and imagine a bigger pay stub, in spite of what it actually says on the one you're holding, you are now changing the cause and you trigger a series of opportunities or events that, if you act on them, will lead you to a higher pay, a bigger pay stub. I say this from personal experience. I've been in the situation where I was looking at my paycheck, imagined it was higher, and opportunities started pouring in. But if you find this hard to believe, I suggest you give it a go. Take your next pay stub, read the amount, and then add something that is believable to your mind. Then close your eyes and give thanks for the new amount you want to see on your pay stub. Move yourself on the frequency of already having received the higher amount and be grateful as if you have already been paid that. And if you care to share your experience, I would love to hear from you; email me at silviu@arenes.pro.

Giving thanks to the universe or to a god for the wonder of your life, and for what you want to bring about in your reality, moves mountains, travels the universe through time and space, and raises you to the frequency associated with that gratitude where you can see and grasp more of it. But there is another way you can use gratitude to enrich your life and that is by giving thanks to the people you meet in your day-to-day life. And I'm not talking about throwing a "thanks" to the barista that made you a coffee, the waiter that brought you the menu, or the person who held the door for you. I'm talking about bringing the energy of gratitude to the forefront of your awareness whenever you can. Take a moment to look that person in the eye and realize that no matter how small that gesture they did for you, they chose to do it, and for that they deserve your gratitude and a "Thank You!" And feel that gratitude – feel that built up energy – leaving your body and embracing that person.

In doing so, you're not just making that person feel appreciated and encouraging them to be a better person. In doing so, you start a ripple effect, like throwing a stone in the water that makes ripples all the way to the other end of the shore. That ripple effect will start bouncing from this person onto the next one, and then on to the next one, all the way to the other side of the world. When you propel your gratitude energy through the people you meet, you surround the whole world with that energy. You're embracing the whole world with your love, and that energy has no other way to go but back into your very being. Some people say that you can't change the world on your own – I believe you can. It may not be that impactful for the world at large, but it will be enough for the person you're showing your love and gratitude to, and since that person is part of the world, the world has changed a little bit thanks to your action.

The feeling that you get from giving genuine gratitude to another human being is the highest form of love and appreciation for yourself, as you see yourself in that other human being. Gratitude does more than changing your perspective to allow you to see the world from a different point of view; it improves your health and wealth, your relationships, your interactions with the outside world, and so much more. When you are consistently grateful for things you see and things you imagine, you move yourself to the frequency of receiving more of the things you are grateful for. Being happy doesn't mean you have it all; it simply means being thankful for all you have.

Ho'oponopono

Ho'oponopono is a traditional Hawaiian practice of reconciliation and forgiveness that has gained popularity as a spiritual healing technique in modern times. The word "ho'oponopono" roughly translates to "to make right" or "to rectify an error" in Hawaiian. Historically, ho'oponopono was used by Hawaiian families or communities to resolve conflicts, restore harmony, and promote healing. It involved gathering together to discuss and address issues, express forgiveness, and release negative emotions. The process typically included prayers, chants, and rituals facilitated by a respected elder or practitioner.

In recent decades, Dr. Ihaleakala Hew Len, a Hawaiian psychologist, introduced a modern adaptation of ho'oponopono known as "Self-Identity through Ho'oponopono."[30] Dr. Len's approach emphasizes personal responsibility and the idea that external experiences are reflections of our own inner state of being.

The core principle of ho'oponopono, as taught by Dr. Len and others, is based on the belief that we are responsible for everything in our lives, including our thoughts, actions, and experiences. According to this perspective, when we encounter challenges or conflicts in our lives, they are manifestations of unresolved issues within ourselves. Therefore, to heal and transform our external realities, we must first address and release the inner beliefs, memories, and emotions that are contributing to the problem.

The practice of ho'oponopono involves four key phrases or mantras:

I love you – affirming love and compassion for oneself and for others, recognizing the interconnectedness of all beings and the healing power of love.

I'm sorry – expressing remorse and taking responsibility for whatever issue or conflict is present, even if we're not fully aware of its origins.

Please forgive me – requesting forgiveness from a higher power or from the collective consciousness for any errors or negative energies that have contributed to the situation.

Thank you – expressing gratitude for the opportunity to heal and release old patterns or memories.

These phrases are repeated silently or aloud as a form of prayer or meditation, with the intention of clearing and transmuting negative energies and promoting healing and reconciliation. Ho'oponopono is often practiced as a form of self-healing and spiritual growth, but it can also be used to address conflicts in relationships, heal trauma, and cultivate inner peace and harmony. While its effectiveness may vary from person to person, many practitioners, myself included, experience profound shifts in their lives and relationships through consistent practice.

I've been practicing ho'oponopono for years now. My life has been transformed, and I feel light and happy. Every event that drags my energy down is now a trigger that reminds me that I am the cause of that event. I am there and I am experiencing that event because I caused it somehow. I don't always know how I did it, but I do have the belief that I am the cause of my own life with all that comes my way, and for this reason alone I am responsible to cleanse it. The reckless driver, the angry customer, or the annoying colleague – whatever it is – has come my way because at one point I put myself on that frequency and pulled that person or event into my life, so now it's my responsibility. I use this as a trigger to chant, "I love you. I'm sorry. Please forgive me. Thank you." When I do this I feel better and lighter; I accept whatever it is for what is and move on.

Mindfulness

At its core, mindfulness involves being consciously aware of what is happening within and around you, embracing the present moment without judgement or resistance, and the acceptance of your thoughts, emotions, and bodily sensations, fully engaging with the present moment, rather than dwelling on the past or worrying about the future. The concept of mindfulness has deep roots in ancient Eastern philosophical and religious traditions, particularly within Buddhism. However, the modern understanding and application of mindfulness have been shaped by a convergence of various cultural and historical influences.

Mindfulness (known as "sati" in Pali, the language of the earliest Buddhist scriptures) is a central aspect of Buddhist teachings. The Buddha emphasized mindfulness as a fundamental practice on the path to enlightenment. In early Buddhist texts such as the Satipatthana Sutta (Discourse on the Foundations of Mindfulness)[31], mindfulness is described as a way to observe and understand the nature of existence, including the impermanence of phenomena and the workings of the mind.

As Buddhism spread throughout Asia, mindfulness practices evolved and diversified within various Buddhist schools and traditions. Techniques such as breath awareness, body scanning, and mindful movement became integral parts of meditation practices across different cultures and regions. Beyond Buddhism, mindfulness-like practices can be found in other contemplative traditions, including Hinduism, Taoism, and various indigenous spiritual practices. These traditions also emphasize present-moment awareness, introspection, and the cultivation of inner peace.

The modern revival of mindfulness in the West can be traced back to the mid-20th century. Jon Kabat-Zinn, a professor of medicine, developed the Mindfulness-Based Stress Reduction (MBSR)[32] program in 1979, which adapted mindfulness meditation for alleviating stress, chronic pain, and various psychological conditions.

The 21st century witnessed a surge of scientific research exploring the effects of mindfulness on mental and physical health. Studies have demonstrated its effectiveness in reducing stress, anxiety, depression, and improving cognitive function, emotional regulation, and overall well-being.[33] This empirical evidence has contributed to the widespread adoption of mindfulness-based interventions in clinical settings, schools, workplaces, and beyond.

Today, mindfulness has become a mainstream practice embraced by people from diverse backgrounds seeking greater mental clarity, emotional balance, and inner peace amidst the complexities of modern life. Its integration into various fields – from psychology and education to business and sports – reflects its universal appeal and enduring relevance in fostering human flourishing.

The practice of mindfulness offers a wide range of benefits that positively impact various aspects of mental, emotional, and physical well-being. Mindfulness has been shown to reduce stress by promoting relaxation and helping individuals develop a more adaptive response to stressors. By cultivating present-moment awareness, individuals can break the cycle of rumination and worry that often exacerbate stress.

It helps us develop greater awareness of our emotions without becoming overwhelmed by them. This awareness enables better regulation of emotions, leading to decreased reactivity and increased resilience in the face of challenging situations. Regular mindfulness practice strengthens the ability to sustain attention and concentrate on tasks, leading to improved productivity and performance in various domains, such as work, study, and daily activities.

Mindfulness cultivates a deeper understanding of our thoughts, feelings, and behavioral patterns. This self-awareness fosters personal growth, self-acceptance, and the ability to make conscious choices aligned with our values and goals. It promotes a non-judgmental attitude toward oneself and others, fostering greater compassion, empathy, and understanding. By cultivating an open-hearted presence, we develop stronger interpersonal connections and contribute to creating more harmonious relationships.

The practice of mindfulness helps alleviate insomnia and improve sleep quality by calming the mind, reducing nighttime rumination, and promoting relaxation. Improved sleep contributes to overall well-being and vitality.

By cultivating a present-moment awareness and developing a non-reactive stance toward life's challenges, mindfulness fosters the ability to bounce back from adversity and adapt to change with greater ease. Research suggests that mindfulness practices may have positive effects on various aspects of physical health, including immune function, cardiovascular health, and inflammation levels. It may also support healthier lifestyle choices, such as mindful eating and regular physical activity.

Mindfulness can be cultivated through various practices, such as meditation, body scan, deep breathing exercises, mindful movement (such as yoga or tai chi), active listening, journaling, and simply by intentionally bringing awareness to everyday activities like eating, walking, driving, washing dishes, and so on.

Incorporating These Tools into Your Daily Life

My day actually starts in the evening. Neville Goddard's teachings[34] suggest that the moments before sleep are particularly potent for influencing our experiences of the following day. He claims that visualizing your next day imprints your subconscious mind and the universe at large with those images, which influence the events of the following day.

I choose to start my day every evening by falling asleep to the ho'oponopono practice. As I close my eyes and drift off to sleep, I repeat the four magic phrases over and over in my mind – I love you. I'm sorry. Please forgive me. Thank you. It cleanses my day of any negativity that I may have encountered, allowing for a deep resting sleep, and it cleans the slate for the day that follows, giving me the opportunity to start afresh.

As soon as I wake up in the morning, before I open my eyes, I start giving thanks for all the things and people in

Does this assume you are wrong/ acting badly, looking for forgiveness of what?

my life. Some things are consistent every morning like gratitude for my life, for my wife, my health and wealth, my home and business, and my family and friends. Some things change based on the plans I have for the day, for instance, if I have a meeting, I give thanks for a great outcome, if I have a trip to make, I give thanks for the safe journey ahead, and so on. As I get out of bed, I bring my awareness to my senses and I feel gratitude for the little things: the comfort of the bed, the texture of the sheets, the soft touch of the carpet under my feet, running water, soap, and so on.

The next thing I do is drink a pint of water. Throughout the night, our bodies lose water through breathing and sweating. Drinking water upon waking helps replenish the body's fluid levels, and it prevents dehydration, which can lead to symptoms such as fatigue, headaches, and difficulty concentrating. Drinking water in the morning helps jumpstart our metabolisms. Studies have shown that it increases our metabolic rates, which may also help us burn more calories throughout the day, if that is something that you're focusing on.

Drinking water upon waking also helps flush out toxins and waste products that have accumulated in your body overnight. This promotes kidney function and supports the body's natural detoxification processes. Water helps stimulate digestion and hydrates the brain, and it improves alertness, focus, and mental clarity. It hydrates your skin from the inside out, lubricates joints, reduces inflammation, and alleviates discomfort associated with conditions like arthritis or muscle soreness. Plenty of reasons to have that pint of water.

After this I start my exercises. I don't spend too much time on this because I get to walk and run a lot throughout the day, but I do enough to get my blood pumping and the adrenaline kick that gives me the feel-good feeling and the energy to start the day. If you're in an office job and don't get much exercise, I highly recommend a good thirty minutes workout, but if you're new to this, start small; start with whatever you can and add a bit more the next day, and so on, until you get to at least thirty minutes, and remember – consistency is the key.

Next, I mix affirmations with mindfulness by writing in an A4 notebook as mentioned earlier when I was talking about affirmations. Our minds tend to wander when doing a repetitive thing, so when I sense that I am no longer present when writing, I bring myself to the present moment by attempting slow calligraphic writing so that I can feel the pen touching the paper, hear it scratching, and smell that ink. As I get toward the bottom of the page, I start writing with my non-dominant hand. It forces my mind to focus on that activity, and it engages my brain in a challenging task, stimulating neural pathways and promoting brain plasticity (the process of change of the nervous system as a result of intrinsic factors, environmental inputs, learning experiences, or lesions)[35]. This also helps enhance cognitive function, improve coordination, and maintain brain health.

As a bonus, writing with the non-dominant hand can activate different areas of the brain associated with creativity and intuition. This can encourage divergent thinking and help overcome creative blocks, leading to fresh insights and ideas. Long term, it helps improve dexterity and coordination in both hands, and it can improve problem-solving abilities and cognitive flexibility. It encourages the brain to adapt to new situations and find creative solutions to challenges. Some people find that writing with the non-dominant hand allows them to access deeper emotions and insights that may be less accessible through conventional writing, and it can gradually improve ambidexterity. This can be advantageous in various activities and occupations that require manual dexterity and coordination.[36]

Once this process is complete, I carry on with my daily activity, trying to be as mindful and present in all activities. As I make the coffee, I give thanks for the ingredients, enjoy the smell of roasted coffee, and give thanks for all the people who worked tirelessly to bring that coffee into my home. As I grab the sugar, I carry on with the thanks, and so on. Washing the dishes is one of my favorite tasks as I get to feel the warmth of the water and enjoy the squeaky clean sensation of the freshly washed tableware.

Throughout the day, as I drive, I pay particular attention to the texture of the wheel drive, and being present in the experience very often allows me to foresee and prevent incidents. In the moments that I don't do it and I find myself enraged by a "running late" driver swerving in my lane, I start repeating the ho'oponopono mantra – I love you. I'm sorry. Please forgive me. Thank you. I acknowledge that I create my day and I am responsible for everything that happens around me including that individual. Once I've calmed down and relaxed, I turn back to being mindful on a safe journey. With every opportunity I have throughout the day, I either listen to an audiobook or open my kindle app and read a few pages from whatever book I am reading. Educating myself is as important as exercise, gratitude, mindfulness, affirmations, drinking water, and breathing.

In the evening, I reward myself with some unwinding time. This involves spending time with my wife, cooking dinner, enjoying the dinner, and then watching sitcoms that make me laugh. When bedtime comes, I grab a book and read until I can no longer concentrate. Then I close my eyes and start chanting the ho'oponopono.

This is but an example of a day in my life. You can tailor your day however you find it suitable to your schedule, but make sure you incorporate as many of these tools as you can – they are the key to finding your happiness.

Afterward

The tools presented in this book have helped me tremendously throughout the years, and my only hope is that they will serve you well in your search for peace and happiness. If you enjoyed reading this book and found the information useful, please help me to help other people in their search for happiness. I only wish to spread the joy throughout the world, and I can only do it with your help.

Be kind to yourself!

Be kind to the people you love!

Be kind to all the people you meet!

If you are kind, that kindness kindles hope in the hearts of those you touch, and it shares the light with those that are further touched by it. We are energy conductors; whatever energy comes to us gets passed on to the next person. Choose to touch people with kindness so they can pass on that kindness further.

And if you want to do more than that, please leave a review on the website you purchased this book. Your words will help others make an informed decision. Share it on social media!

Furthermore, gift this book to those you love and you think would benefit from the info that's in it. Help them find their happiness.

And finally, if you want to help even more, please help me decide on the topic of the next book in this series. I plan on diving deeper into all aspects of life; whether it's relationships, parenthood, financial, or work-related, your say will help me prioritize the subject of the next book, and once that's published, you'll be the first to know. Simply email me at *silviu@arenes.pro* with the subject "Next Book" and let me know what you want to learn more about.

In the meantime, while I'm working on the new release, check out my other book – *YOU and Your Own Universe*, available on Amazon UK, scan this code with your phone:

this one for the rest of the world:

or search online *YOU and Your Own Universe* and see what is available in your area.

Acknowledgments

First and foremost, I extend my heartfelt gratitude to you, my dear reader. You are the very reason this book has come into existence. As discussed throughout these pages, we attract into our lives what resides within us. While we may not always manifest our thoughts directly, we share them with the world on a quantum level. I merely picked up the idea from you and shaped it into the form you now hold in your hands. So, thank you!

I would also like to express my deep appreciation to Victoria Seymour of SEYMOUR PROOFREADING for her exceptional work. As you might have gathered from the content of this book, English is not my first language, and I am truly grateful for her invaluable input.

A heartfelt thank you to all my clients and colleagues across various industries. Your perspectives have enriched my understanding of the world.

My deepest gratitude goes to the authors whose books I have read throughout my life. Your words have profoundly shaped my mind.

Lastly, but certainly not least, I want to thank my beloved wife, Roxana. For the past 23 years, she has stood by my side through all the ups and downs.

References

[1] Clear, J. (2018). *Atomic Habits*, [Audiobook]. Retrieved from https://www.amazon.co.uk/gp/product/1847941834

[2] Hamel, G., Prahalad, C.K., (1996). *Competing for the Future*. https://www.amazon.co.uk/dp/0875847161

[3] Maslow, A., (1943) *A Theory of Human Motivation*, Psychological Review, 50, 370-396.
https://psychclassics.yorku.ca/Maslow/motivation.htm

[4] Ruiz, Don M., (2005). *The Four Agreements*, [Audiobook]. Retrieved from https://www.amazon.co.uk/dp/B002SQ45B4/

[5] Nightingale Conant Learning System. (2009). *The Richest Man in Babylon... In Action*. [Audiobook]. Retrieved from https://www.amazon.co.uk/gp/product/B00N4LI5S6/

[6] The Dhammapada, *The Buddha's Path to Wisdom*, Chapter 1, Art. 2, https://www.buddhanet.net/e-learning/buddhism/dp01.htm

[7] Goodreads, https://www.goodreads.com/quotes/620707

[8] Secrets of Success, *64 Best P.T. Barnum Quotes of All Time to Get Inspired*, https://www.secretsofsuccess.com/blog/best-pt-barnum-quotes

[9] Brainy Quote, https://www.brainyquote.com/quotes/groucho_marx_157474

[10] Emerald Tablet, https://en.wikipedia.org/wiki/Emerald_Tablet

[11] Twitter, Eckhart Tolle profile, https://x.com/EckhartTolle/status/1349714162553909248

[12] Wattles, W. D., (1911). *The Science of Being Great*, The Elizabeth Towne Company, Chapter 8, p. 49

[13] Russell, B., (1929). *Marriage and Morals*, Liveright Publishing Corporation, Chapter 19, p. 96

[14] Hawkins, D. R. PhD. (1995), *Power vs. Force: The Hidden Determinants of Human Behaviour*, Veritas Publishing

[15] Brainy Quote, https://www.brainyquote.com/quotes/rabindranath_tagore_388896

[16] The Holy Bible. (2011). New International Version. https://www.bible.com/en-GB/

[17] Goodreads, https://www.goodreads.com/author/quotes/7268.Jimi_Hendrix

[18] Goodreads, https://www.goodreads.com/quotes/694816

[19] Brainy Quote, https://www.brainyquote.com/quotes/buddha_104025

[20] Goodreads, https://www.goodreads.com/quotes/95476

[21] The Holy Bible. (2011). New International Version. https://www.bible.com/en-GB/

[22] Talmud, Shabbat 31a-b, https://steinsaltz.org/daf/shabbat31/

[23] Hadith 13, 40 Hadith an-Nawawi, https://sunnah.com/nawawi40:13

[24] Analects 12:2, https://confucius.page/analects-12-2/

[25] Rockhill, W. Woodville, (1883) *Udanavarga*, Trubner & Co., Ludgate Hill, Chapter 5, Verse 18, p27, https://archive.org/details/in.ernet.dli.2015.283948

[26] Goodreads, https://www.goodreads.com/quotes/37815

[27] Online Etymology Dictionary, https://www.etymonline.com/word/educate

[28] Goodreads, https://www.goodreads.com/quotes/536931

[29] Goodreads, https://www.goodreads.com/quotes/17490

[30] Radhe, K. (n.d.). *Ihaleakala Hew Len PhD. And Ho'Oponopono. Dr. Len's Amazing Success with Ho'Oponopono.* Blue Bottle Love.
https://www.bluebottlelove.com/hew-len-hooponopono/

[31] Wikipedia, *Satipatthana Sutta,*
https://en.wikipedia.org/wiki/Satipatthana_Sutta

[32] National Library of Medicine, *Mindfulness-based stress reduction: a non-pharmacological approach for chronic illnesses,* Introduction,
https://www.ncbi.nlm.nih.gov/pmc/articles/PMC3336928/

[33] Madhav Goyal, MD, MPH; Sonal Singh, MD, MPH; Erica M. S. Sibinga, MD, MHS; et al, JAMA Internal Medicine, (2014), *Meditation Programs for Psychological Stress and Well-being,*
https://jamanetwork.com/journals/jamainternalmedicine/fullarticle/1809754

[34] Goddard, N. (2015). *Feeling Is the Secret* [Audiobook]. Retrieved from https://www.amazon.co.uk/gp/product/B00ZGHC1IG/

[35] Fatima Y. Ismail, Milos R. Ljubisavljevic, Michael V. Johnston, Handbook of Clinical Neurology, Chapter 6 - A conceptual framework for plasticity in the developing brain, Volume 173, 2020, Pages 57-66,
https://www.sciencedirect.com/science/article/abs/pii/B9780444641502

[36] Benjamin A. Philip, Scott H. Frey, Increased functional connectivity between cortical hand areas and praxis network associated with training-related improvements in non-dominant hand precision drawing, Neuropsychologia, Volume 87, 1 July 2016, Pages 157-168,
https://www.sciencedirect.com/science/article/abs/pii/S0028393216301671

Milton Keynes UK
Ingram Content Group UK Ltd.
UKHW021828270924
448907UK00009B/206